Corporate Tax Evasion and Governments

European University Studies

Europäische Hochschulschriften
Publications Universitaires Européennes

Series V
Economics and Management

Reihe V Série V
Volks- und Betriebswirtschaft
Sciences économiques, gestion d'entreprise

Vol./Bd. 3265

PETER LANG
Frankfurt am Main · Berlin · Bern · Bruxelles · New York · Oxford · Wien

Julia Kupzowa

Corporate Tax Evasion and Governments

Analysis and Policy Implications for Russia

PETER LANG
Internationaler Verlag der Wissenschaften

Bibliographic Information published by the Deutsche Nationalbibliothek
The Deutsche Nationalbibliothek lists this publication in the Deutsche Nationalbibliografie; detailed bibliographic data is available in the internet at <http://www.d-nb.de>.

Zugl.: Erlangen, Nürnberg Univ., Diss., 2006

Printed with financial support of the
Konrad-Adenauer-Stiftung.

n2
ISSN 0531-7339
ISBN 978-3-631-56627-5

Preface

Tax evasion still remains a very acute problem in Russia as well as in other countries although the underlying problems may be quite different in developed, developing and transition economics. The specific of tax evasion in transition economies such as Russia is that corruptive and extortive governments are responsible for the part of tax evasion. For example, tighter grip of the "bad state" causes extortion which increases the level of tax evasion.

The analysis of the causes of tax evasion in Russia and the corresponding policy implications are the aim of this thesis.

It is a pleasure to acknowledge people who have helped in making my dissertation better. First of all, I would like to thank my supervisor, Prof. Dr. Berthold Wigger for giving impulse to explore this subject as well as for his constant support during my stay at his chair. Many thanks also to my second corrector Prof. Dr. Wolfram Reiss for the discussion and the helpful comments.

I am particularly grateful to Dr. Ralph C. Bayer for the collaborative research which we started during my research semester at the University of Adelaide and which contributed to the development of my dissertation.

My thanks are due to my colleagues at the chair of Public Finance of the Friedrich-Alexander University of Erlangen-Nuremberg, Robert Dehm, Daniel Frohschammer, Alexander von Kotzebue, Dr. Frank Kupferschmidt, Dr. Jobst Leikeb und Dr. Udo Wartha, who read and commented on the final draft of the thesis and were supportive friends all the time I spent in Nuremberg.

I would especially like to acknowledge the financial and personal support of the Konrad-Adenauer Fund which made my PhD. studies in Germany possible.

Finally, I want to thank my husband, Dmitri Fedossov, who encouraged me and supported in this endeavor and to whom I devote this book.

Nuremberg, March 2007 Julia Kupzowa

Contents

List of Tables

List of Figures

List of abbreviations

CIS	Commonwealth of Independent States
GDP	Gross Domestic Product
GNP	Gross National Product
IMF	International Monetary Fund
NPV	Net Present Value
OECD	Organization of Economic Cooperation and Development
RUR	Russian Ruble
SNA	Statistics of National Accounts
USD	US-Dollar
VAT	Value Added Tax
WSIOM	Russian Center for Public Opinion Study

Chapter 1

Introduction

1.1 Motivation, purpose and structure

From the beginning of transition in Russia the level of tax evasion has increased significantly, from 14.7 in 1990 to 45.1 percent of GDP in 2000-01[1]. Being quite high, these figures indicate inefficiencies in tax collection. Admitting this problem's existence the government has taken steps to improve the situation by introducing tax reform which reduced both the number of taxes and their rates. Although having some positive effects, the taken measures didn't considerably reduce the evasion of firms' main taxes[2]. High evasion of profit tax, especially among natural resource companies, as well as the underreporting of payroll, are still to be observed.

Taking into account the importance of the problem, the analysis focuses on specifics which better explain tax evasion in Russia and proposes some policy implications.

Since most individuals in Russia pay their taxes on a withholding basis, firms are responsible for the greatest part of tax evasion. Thus we concentrate here on the tax evasion of firms. The theoretical as well as empirical literature on this particular topic is scarce since the economic approach is focused on individual decisions about tax evasion.

Furthermore, explicit country distinctions are seldom made[3], although country specific determinants of tax evasion exist. A transition economy as Russia provides an example that tax evasion is more than just onesided cheating of the government. It is a rather complicated process involving various agents and caused by particular policy and pace of development.

[1] See Schneider, F. and Enste, D., 2003.

[2] See Gurvich, E., 2004.

[3] See Gerxhani, K., 2004, p.294.

Thus, privatization in Russia introduced specific kind of relations between the state and business where the incentives to evade taxes were exacerbated.

Tax evasion in Russia is accompanied by corruption and extortion. There is, in particular little research on the last aspect, whereby it has become acute for Russia. Russian business reported a significant increase in the extortive activities last year[4]. Such practices provide evidence of the failure to build rapport between the state and society. The situation is also quite specific in Russia in this respect. Business is the main taxpayer as well as tax evader. Society in its turn blames the state for the inability to provide public goods.

All these issues suggest the reconsideration of standard policy measures to fight tax evasion, primarily penalties and auditing but also tax rates[5].

In recent years it has often been emphasized that the functioning of formal institutions in a country can explain the extent of tax evasion. The Russian case of firms' evasion proves this hypothesis. The failure of the state to guarantee property rights and to provide fair treatment under the rule of law are evident. Tax evasion, as we will show, is greatly influenced by these factors. Our analysis will try to shed light on particular economic and institutional development in Russia.

The purpose of this thesis is to analyze and model the Russian-specific features of tax evasion as well as the existing mechanisms. It focusses mainly on the role of governments and their policies towards tax evasion of Russian enterprise.

In the second chapter we focus on the main economic and non-economic factors which cause tax evasion in Russia. Analysis of the scale of tax evasion based on surveys measuring the underground economy in Russia will also help to define the most important determinants of tax evasion. The mechanisms as well the realized policy measures are evaluated.

The third chapter reviews the relevant theoretical literature on tax evasion and draws conclusions which can be inferred from them. In the third chapter we model the Russian-specific features of tax evasion. Firstly the model of tax evasion and corruption is presented, then we concentrate on extortion issues. The static game is introduced where nature draws the type of government: good or bad. Then we extend the model by introducing the dynamic game where additionally the type of firm (its profitability) is determined by nature. Subsequently we analyze the situation when extortion is costly to the government.

[4]See the MosNews' website for further details (www.mosnews.com/news/2005/03/28/pubusiness.shtml).

[5]On the complementary nature of corruption and tax evasion and corresponding policy measures see Cule, M. and Fulton, M., 2005.

In the fourth chapter we present the formal conditions of firm's evasion and offer the mechanism which alleviates potential incentives for cost and profit distortions. We conclude with a numerical example on this issue.

Chapter 5 concludes with policy implications where tax policy and institutional recommendations are proposed.

Chapter 2

Positive analysis of tax evasion in Russia

2.1 Overview of the Russian current tax features

For more than eight years Russia has been trying to form a consistent tax system under the Russian Tax Code. The first part came into force in 1999 and determines the general regulations of the country's tax system. Some articles of the second (special) part of the Tax Code regulating specific taxes have been consequently accepted since 2001. The special part has come into operation in 2004, thus completing the establishment of the whole tax system in Russia.

The changes made in the Code are assumed to solve the following main problems: creation of a harmonized and transparent tax system, provision of system's fairness, development of fiscal federalism. A consequence of the Tax Code's adoption is the reduction of the whole number of taxes set from 48 to 26 (previously there were more than 100). Moreover, five special tax regimes were introduced which simplified the tax system to paying one "universal" tax. From a qualitative point of view, the unification of taxes, including those with the similar tax base, improves the function of the common economic environment, contributes to the barrier-free movement of goods and production factors. Special tax regimes foresee a united tax on imputed income for some activities (e.g. agriculture), and a simplified tax system for small corporations, individual taxpayers and mine workings of unused and non-profitable oil-wells.

Today 9 out of 23 taxes foreseen in the Tax Code are closely connected with the use of natural and mineral resources. But these payments made up only 13 percent of all tax revenues in the consolidated budget of 2003[1],[2]. Companies which possess rich natural reserves may make abnormally high profits without considerable financial, technological or labor costs. Therefore the world tax practice shows, that taxation of income from rents[3] contributes to the optimization of tax system and to stable development of the economy. Differentiated rents are the basis of budget revenues in Norway, Arabic countries, some states in the USA and Canada. Introduction of rents' payment for mineral resource usage appears to be an objective necessity for Russia.

The tax on mineral extraction, accepted by the Code and introduced in 2002, provides no income equalization for companies extracting under different economic, geographic and geological conditions. Furthermore, the tax itself is rather primitive. The oil business has lobbied for the temporal character of the tax rate on oil. Its calculation was made according to the transfer prices used by vertically integrated companies which are far away from real market prices. Such a tax practice severely distorts the fairness of competition, putting those companies exploiting richer and more accessible fields in an absolute privileged position.

From this perspective, some economists propose to depart from the existing system of taxation and turn to the taxation of rents. There is an opinion that the appropriate taxation of rents from natural resources would double the budget income. Rents constitute a significant share of GDP, but the fair calculation of rents can be quite complicated. The deposits of natural resources should be properly valued, taking into account the existing pricing in Russia: income from rents within the country is much smaller than from export. Thus it is necessary to differentiate the taxation of rents for inner suppliers and exporters[4].

Some changes were made in the Code concerning income tax. In order to ease the tax burden on wages, a new single tax rate of 13 percent instead of the previously applied progressive scale was introduced. It quickly proved a success in increasing tax revenues, releasing most people from the need to present an annual declaration[5]. Furthermore, in 2001 the authorities introduced a new unified social tax with a regressive scale, which replaced payments to four state social off-budget funds. These two measures have been aimed primarily at stimulating the legalization of organizations' real payrolls thus broadening the base of these taxes.

---

[1]See Panskov, V., 2003, p.103.

[2]Due to the rise in oil prices this share has increased.

[3]Under rents we will understand here inframarginal profits.

[4]See Panskov, V., 2003, p.111.

[5]Overview: progress of tax reform, Ministry of Taxation of the Russian Federation, October 2003.

Inside the CIS countries VAT calculation has been adjusted to international practice by introducing the principle of destination. Excises on diesel, car oils and gas have been determined; excise rates on gasoline have been considerably increased.

There will be only five local taxes left in the second part of the Tax Code, two of which go in full amount to local budgets. Many local taxes have been abolished. In order to back the revenue level of local budgets the certain shares of profit tax and personal income taxes are provided.

The changes have also been adopted in corporate income taxation. A 35 percent top rate of profit tax has been reduced to 24 percent. Regional authorities can also lower their part of the profit tax not more than on 4 percentage points, from 16 to 12 percent. Moreover, it reduced the tax base since more costs can be considered deductible thus diminishing before-tax profits. In that way tax-adjusted profits approximate to accounting profits. The loss carry-forward provisions were also extended and made less restrictive. Now losses can be carried forward ten years and be offset by up to 30 percent of taxable profit in a given year. At the same time all tax advantages have been formally repealed from 2002. The Code has also managed to abolish the taxes levied on gross income rather than profits which were particularly unpopular[6]. From 2004 the authorities also repealed a sales tax.

The Russian Tax Code hasn't solved the problem of legal and normative documents' unification. More than 120 amendments were adopted in the first half of the year of the Code's functioning. The tasks of the reductions of the whole tax burden, the number of taxes, favors and their regulation, which were implemented in the Code, are not enough for tax reform. Tax reforms are measures to restore the discrepancy between existing tax relations and changing conditions of economic, social and political reality. The above-mentioned tasks can be thus considered from another point of view. For example, the decrease in the number of taxes was implemented, taking into account its influence only on the federal budget. As a result, the existing inefficient and insufficiently elaborated system of fiscal federalism continues the praxis of revenue concentration in the federal budget, extends the praxis of subsidies, while forming regional and local budgets. After the complete adoption of the second part of the Tax Code, local budgets will have only a small number of own taxes (land tax, advertisement tax and the real estate tax) and local fees and charges in full amounts. The "Programme of the Development of Fiscal Federalism in Russian in the period till 2005" also contains personal income tax and corporation profit tax as shared taxes with the federal governments. These two shared taxes are the main tax revenue

[6]The Russian Tax Code, 2000, Part 2, Chapter 25.

sources of regional and local budgets. Taking into account that their total share in the federal tax revenues are quite small (7.79 percent in 2005) the own revenue sources of subnational budgets are negligible. They get the rest as intergovernmental transfers[7].

Summing up the results of the tax reform we underline the following:
1. The rates of the main taxes were reduced.
2. Many taxes were repealed, including the so called turnover taxes.
3. Tax favors were abolished, including the investment credit.
4. The resource sector, especially oil and gas industries are now taxed more heavily, due to the new tax on mineral extraction and export duty.

The reform was carried out following the common opinion that tax burden, particularly on labor, was very high in Russia which leads to the tax evasion and impedes the economic growth. Consequently, the reforms should reduce the level of evasion and accelerate growth, contributing to the recovery of budget losses.

2.2 Scale of tax evasion

Trying to estimate the level of tax evasion inevitably leads to measurement of the shadow economy. According to many authors on this problem (Feige, Frey, Lubell, Pommerehne, Schneider), all economic activities, which contribute to GNP, but are unregistered, are executed in the shadow economy. Consequently, income generated from this production is not reported to tax authorities and tax evasion finds its channel in the economy.

These authors explain shadow economy existence predominantly by three factors: high tax burden (especially income and social security taxes), increased regulation (including regulations on the labor market) and low tax morale due to lack of confidence in public institutions. These three main causes were modelled by Schneider and Enste (2003) to estimate the size of shadow economy in OECD and transition countries, including Russia. The dynamic multiple-indicators multiple-causes model links the size of the shadow economy as an unobserved variable to the observed indicators that reflect changes in the size of the shadow economy over time. In the first equation the shadow economy enters as a dependent variable, where the causes serve as explanatory variables. In the second equation the shadow economy enters as an explanatory variable, where several indicators capture the presence of the shadow activity. For example, decreased labor participation in

[7] For futher details see Intergovernmental Fiscal Relations - International Experience and the Russian Reform, 2005, p. 70-71.

the official economy may signal the increase of employment in the shadow economy; this displacement, consequently, can depress the growth rate of the official economy; monetary transactions can also increase, thus pointing at the growth of the underground economy.

In Russia the size of shadow economy in percentage of gross domestic product was estimated on average in 1990-93 as 27.8 percent and in 2000-01 as 45.1 percent thus demonstrating an increase of 17.3 percent. Among the selected countries only Georgia and Ukraine demonstrated higher growth rates with an approximately 20 percent increase[8]. Broadly speaking, the size of the shadow economy lies for the transition economies to which Russia belongs in the middle between developed (12 percent) and developing (35-44 percent depending on the region) for the years 1990-1993[9]. But the study demonstrates the growing size of it. Since the tax burden seems to significantly affect the size of shadow economy, recent Russian tax reforms are likely to reduce the scale of underground economy and tax evasion.

As can be seen at first sight, the aim of the tax rates' reduction and thus the tax burden is achieved to some extent with the introduction of the Tax Code. According to the estimation of the tax burden as a ratio of all taxes received from taxpayers to the gross domestic product of the country, for Russia this ratio was 35.4 percent in 2001[10], less than for most developed European countries and the East European economies which underwent more successful transition (Czech Republic, Hungary, Slovenia). After the tax reform and the Tax Code's provisions this index is expected to be even less. But we should be accurate about this statement for following reasons.

The calculations, which are applicable and transparent for the developed countries, must be considered carefully for the Russian tax system, taking into account the peculiarities of Russian economy's development at the current stage. Detailed analysis of these features provides some corrections to the index and gives evidence that the situation is much more complicated than it seems at first sight. To outline only the three above mentioned causes for the growth of the shadow economy is not enough to capture Russian reality.

Let us consider the factors which distort the index of tax burden in the Russian tax system. According to Tax Ministry information, approximately one in six taxpayers pays due taxes to the budget punctually and in full. Approximately half of taxpayers pays, but at the same time minimizes tax duties legally and illegally. The others prefer not paying taxes: some tax-

[8]Schneider, F., Enste, D., 2003, p.37.
[9]ibid., p.37.
[10]See Panskov, V., 2003, p.72.

payers present the so called "zero bottom lines"; some do not register with the tax authorities. The Ministry of Finance estimates that some 30 to 50 percent of taxes are lost annually for the consolidated budget[11]. Hence, honest taxpayers pay taxes according to the part of GDP produced only in the official economy. This argument can be partly captured as low tax morale and characterizes the firms operating in the shadow economy.

Secondly, tax duties and their fulfillment are not the same in the Russian economy. Put it differently, such a taxpayer is used to paying as much as he wants or can, or is able to agree with the government, but not as supposed by the law. Government bodies stimulated this practice by offering tax payers a form of trade-off by which a taxpayer could pay only part of the tax and the rest of the tax due was considered as a tax liability which was often paid in non-monetary form later. As a result of the huge tax arrears the authorities were compelled to brisk up the restructuring of enterprises' tax debts in 2000-2001. Nevertheless, to the beginning of 2003, the whole sum of tax arrears made up 37 billion dollars. In this connection, Gaddy and Ickes (1998) claims the existence of the virtual economy in Russia, which also contributes to the growth of tax evasion. In 1995 and 1996, 24 percent of all federal taxes were paid in non-monetary form; in 1997, the non-monetary share was 41 percent. In 1996, the average share of non-monetary tax revenues comprised 60 percent of regional budgets and 43 percent of local budgets (survey made by OECD for a sample of 39 out of 89 regions)[12]. In the last years the situation with tax arrears improved but established praxis had already formed distorted relations between the government and firms as concerned collection of taxes.

Thirdly, the index of tax burden in Russia is also imperfect, because there are considerable errors in GDP measurement. It is impossible to define the quantitative influence of the errors on GDP measuring. The Russian Statistical Committee completes official data by adding up the GDP produced in the shadow economy, estimated at its lowest level of 25 percent. Meanwhile, the shadow economy pays no taxes, but calculation up the sum of unpaid taxes is not carried out. Therefore, the real tax burden of taxpayers must be increased by 25 percent minimum, and 40 percent maximum, and comprises already not 35.4 percent of GDP, but 44.2 to 50 percent[13].

Tax evasion decreases the tax burden for those who evade, but increases it for honest taxpayers. The aim of the reform to reduce the tax rates was to diminish the gap between nominal and effective tax rates by decreasing

[11]Panskov, V., 2003, p.74.

[12]OECD Economic Surveys, Russian Federation 1997, Paris, 1997, p.181.

[13]See Panskov, V., 2003, p.77.

the former and increasing the latter. Nominal tax rates, if compared with the successful East European transition economies, are lower in Russia, but whether the high level of tax evasion could be reduced by lowering the nominal tax rates is not directly obvious. Friedman, Johnson, Kaufmann and Zoido-Lobaton (1999) found in a cross-country analysis that higher tax rates are associated with less unofficial activity as percent of GDP. They argue that firms go into the shadow economy not to avoid official taxes but to reduce the burden of bureaucracy and corruption. So the bargaining game between government and firms plays more role than tax burden. They also found that a one-percent increase in an index of regulation (ranging from 1 to 5) is associated with a 10-percent increase in the shadow economy. Analyzing the relationship between bribery and shadow economy, Johnson, Kaufmann and Zoido-Lobaton found that a one-percent improvement in the index of corruption (ranging from 1 to 7,[14] is associated with an 8-11 percentage point decrease in the shadow economy[15].

To consider the regulations of the labor market in particular, they are not significant for the Russian market and do not influence the level of evasion. Furthermore, there are no observed distortions of individual decisions about the allocation of working hours due, for example, to the negative elasticity of hours worked in the shadow economy with respect to the wage rate in the official sector. The shadow economy's labor force in percentage of working age population coincided roughly with the size of the shadow economy and amounted to 40.9 percent in 1998-99[16].

Yoo and Hyun (1998) proposed the "expenditure-income discrepancy" approach to estimate the size of the shadow economy according to which the income measure of GNP should be equal to the expenditure measure of GNP. Consequently, the existing gap can be considered as a measure of the shadow economy. In Russia this gap in 1995 was estimated at 74.9 percent[17]. The method is criticized for omissions and errors in national accounting and for the accuracy of estimates which are often problematic in transition countries.

The next method with which the shadow economy's estimates in Russia were obtained is the electricity consumption method. It is assumed that the ratio of overall GDP in official and underground economies to electricity consumption (electricity/GDP elasticity is one, for Russia it was 0.9) is constant, so they change together. Consequently, the growth of the whole GDP can be inferred from the growth of the electricity consumption. The difference between the growth rate of the total and official GDP is attributed

[14] A higher score means less corruption. Russia got 2.72.
[15] Johnson, S., Kaufmann, D., Zoido-Lobaton, P., 1998, p.391
[16] Estimation of Schneider, see Schneider, F., Enste, D., 2000
[17] ibid., p.93.

to the growth of the shadow economy. Using the values from Johnson, Kaufmann and Shleifer (1997) Schneider (2000) estimated the shadow economy as 14.7 percent of GDP in 1989-90, 27 percent in 1990-93 and 41 percent in 1994-95[18].

Eilat and Zinnes (2000) got the following estimations: 1990 - 17 percent, 1991 - 18, 1992 - 30, 1993 - 35, 1994 - 45. Johnson, Kaufmann and Zoido-Lobaton (1998) obtained 39 percent in 1990-93 and 69 percent in 1994-95 for Russia. Using the household electricity method, developed by Lacko (1996), the size of the shadow economy averaged, in 1990-93, 36.9 percent and in 1994-95, 39.2 percent, demonstrating only a slight increase[19].

Eilat and Zinnes (2000) modified the electricity consumption method and estimated the Russian shadow economy at 53 percent in 1995, 54 percent in 1996, and 52 percent in 1997[20]. Getting the annual percentage change in electricity consumption from the data, they regressed it against several influence variables to capture possible changes in electricity use (price changes, output structure and efficiency in electricity use). Since the coefficients were statistically significant, these factors should be filtered to remove their influence. They also modified the multiple-indicators multiple-causes model to make it more relevant for transition economies. Firstly, they use only one indicator - unexplained electricity, which was obtained in the previous method by filtering the data of electricity consumption from influenced elements. The unobserved size of the shadow economy to be found enters into the equation as an explanatory variable, on which the indicator is dependant. They also chose another two causes, which better capture the reality of transition: the ability of the government to exercise its fiscal control over the economy (ranging from 0 (least control) to 1 (most control), corruption-regulation variable (ranging from 0 (high corruption, high regulatory burden) to 1 (low corruption, low regulatory burden). Estimating the first cause variable showed that a country that scores perfectly will have a shadow of 17 percent of GDP, and a country that scores the worst will have a shadow of 117 percent of GDP (Russia got 89 percent); for the second cause variable - 10 and 140 percent of GDP (Russia 88 percent) correspondingly. Averaging the predicted values across both cause regressions the size of shadow economy for Russia was estimated as 89 percent of GDP, the highest among all the estimates, but according to the authors - the best reflection of the shadow economy.

In addition to the discussed indirect methods of estimation, direct methods are also used: surveys and interviews as well as tax auditing. Surveys

---

[18] Schneider, F., Enste, D., 2000.

[19] ibid., p.101.

[20] Eilat, Y., Zinnes, C., 2000.

of economic activities and attitudes, although used in exceptions, provide specific characteristics of tax evasion which help not only to estimate their size but to infer particular determinants of the problem.

Researchers from the St. Petersburg State University of Economics and Finance provided a concept of measurement of shadow economic activity at the regional level by identifying shadow flows emerging at every stage of value-adding operations based on the direct method. The respondents (tax and financial authorities, and company accountants) from St. Petersburg provided answers to the questionnaire offering to estimate the extent of particular misreporting for 3 groups (up to 10 percent of shadow activities, 10-20 and 20 and more) of firms in the four main sectors in percentages. The SNA[21]-based approach allowed estimation of the average level of misreporting of the main components of gross value-added: wages, profits and taxes based at the percentages of answers showing the different levels of misreporting. The average level of tax evasion amounted to 49.3 percent, ranging in industry at 49.8 percent, in construction at 46.7, in transport at 52.8 and in trade at 40.6; the average level of wage bill misreporting was 50.4 and 47.1, 67.4, 50.3, 33.5 percent in the corresponding sectors. The failure to report profits is a major component of shadow economy transactions, which was reported by all the respondents. The percentage of unreported profits was estimated at 34.8 and 42.5, 28.6, 44.8, 43.2 in the sectors. The average weighed share of the unreported gross value added was estimated at 42.8 where the sectoral shares were 33.7, 44.2, 72, 52[22]. The results of the survey also suggest that in St. Petersburg 100 percent of companies are engaged in tax evasion to a more or lesser extent[23].

Using the data of the State Statistical Committee based on SNC, Gurvich, E. et al. (2004) analyzed the scale of tax evasion of different taxes. Thus, the share of the evaded payroll was estimated at 28-35 for 1997-2000, the evaded social tax amounted to 4 percent of GDP. 46 percent of income tax was evaded, which accounted for 3 percent of GDP. In 2000 the net profits in the economy comprised 23 percent of GDP whereas the reported net profits of large and middle companies - only 14 percent, the evaded profit tax can be estimated at 2 percent of GDP. Consequently, the evasion level of these three taxes amounted to 9 percent of GDP.

Other surveys provide specific answers concerning particular attitudes of people and firms to specific evasion activities and government policies aimed at combatting tax evasion. They will be considered in the following para-

[21] Statistics of national accounts

[22] The results will be summarized in table 2.1

[23] Yeliseyeva, I., 2002, p.6.

graphs. Although tax evasion is only part of shadow economic activities, estimates of the underground economy provide an indication of the size of missing tax revenues. Consequently, the government tries to improve its revenue-generating capacity mainly through tax reforms which we have already discussed in the first paragraph.

Sachs, Zinnes and Eilat (2000) examined the nine policy areas which could reduce the level of the shadow economy by looking at what government priorities were in the period 1990-97. Among them, only tax reform was statistically positive significant.

Table 2.1 provides the overview of the shadow economy's estimations analyzed in this paragraph.

As can be inferred from the different estimations, the size of the shadow economy and the corresponding scale of tax evasion vary according to the method applied. The scale of shadow economy can be measured mostly indirectly and the preciseness of an estimation depends on the choice of input variables. Therefore it is important to define the relevant causes of tax evasion for the particular economy. On the other hand, based on the estimators of the shadow economies, important determinants of tax evasion can be identified.

The conclusions which can be made are the following:

1. There are many methods to estimate the size of the shadow economy, and the results are arguable.

2. The difference in the size of the shadow economy between countries with different levels and speed of development indicate the country-specific character of the phenomenon of tax evasion.

3. Varying probable observable causes of the existence of the shadow economy provide us with different estimations which can be inferred as indications for the peculiar causes. Thus, labor regulations are not a motive for informalization in Russia, whereas bribery seems to be a very significant cause.

In the following section we will define the specific motives and causes of Russian economic informality.

2.3 Determinants of tax evasion

Many authors have analyzed motives and causes of informalization and development of the shadow economy where the taxable money income is left unreported with the intention to evade taxes [24]. While considering the factors determining tax evasion, one can define the whole set of coherent economic and non-economic ones. Along many common determinants there are specific features which characterize Russian economic development after the collapse of the Soviet Union. Through the privatization mechanism launched shortly after price and trade liberalization accompanied by inflation and other subsequent factors, tax evasion practices were first introduced in the early nineties, escalated in the mid-nineties and since that time broadly applied.

2.3.1 Privatization: the mechanism of realization due to weak and complex legal and institutional framework

Commenced in order to establish property rights over previous state ownership, privatization reduced the power of central government and turned over large national enterprises in the majority of cases to their old managers (known as insider privatization). Three options of privatization were suggested by the government and in all three of them, given the rapid inflation during the relevant period, the prices that insiders were asked to pay for enterprise shares were very low. In this sense, mass privatization really was a give-away operation[25]. The subsequent decentralization gave governments of all levels much discretion, which in times of macroeconomic instability turned into extortion of firms that operated in their jurisdiction. Significant, often unbearable, tax burden and the complexities of the taxation system were used by local authorities as instruments of such extortion.

Owners and managers of the newly privatized enterprises found themselves in an environment lacking capital markets, available debt and laws ensuring appropriate corporate governance practice. Being often unable to adjust to market economy rules, many of them found no better alternative to maximize their wealth than to strip assets.

In 1995, the loan-for-share program aggravated the illegitimacy of privatization by giving control rights over valuable assets (mainly natural resources) to a small group of oligarchs. There were two known main reasons why the government promoted this mechanism: it needed to increase revenues from privatization, but it was difficult due to the growing uncertainty before parliamentary elections and the direct prohibition of oil industry privatization by the Duma. The second reason was that the banks which proposed the pro-

[24] For the references see Gerxhani K. The informal sector in developed and less developed countries: a literature survey, Public Choice 120, September 2004, p.267-300.

[25] Hare, P., Myravjev, A., 2002.

Table 2.1: The size of the shadow economy in Russia, using different approaches (as percentage of GDP)

Author	1990-1993	1994-1995	2000-2001
Indirect methods			
Schneider (multiple indicators multiple causes model – high tax burden, labor market regulation and low tax morale)	27.8		45.1
Schneider (electricity consumption method)	27.0	41.0	
Schneider (household electricity method)	36.9	39.2	
Eilat, Zinnes (electricity consumption method)	35.0	45.0	
Eilat, Zinnes (modified electricity consumption method)		53.0	
Eilat, Zinnes (multiple indicators multiple causes model – unexplained electricity, corruption-regulation variable, ability of the government to exercise fiscal control)		89.0	
Johnson, Kaufmann, Zoido-Lobaton (electricity consumption method)	39.0	69.0	
Yoo, Hyun (expenditure-income discrepancy)		74.9	
Direct methods			
Yelisejeva			49.3
Gurvich			33.0

Sources: Author's presentation using different estimations

gram wanted to gain control over some of the largest Russian companies as cheaply as possible[26]. The scheme was applied to 12 enterprises (half of them were in the oil industry) which were sold through auctions organized by the consortium of the largest Russian banks for over a billion US dollars within a two-month period, just three months before the presidential elections. The non-transparency of the auctions immediately caused a public uproar over privatization, which contributed to the insecurity of property rights until the present time.

The implemented mechanism of privatization as a give-away process of state property to a part of society preserved the strong link between state and non-state activities inherited from the socialist system[27]. Grossman (1982), while analyzing the informal sector in the USSR, pointed at the importance of social networks, which were also extensively used during privatization. Realization of privatization reinforced the informality of relations between the state and firms, giving the firms ways to cheat the government and providing the state with discretion used for tax collection until today.

In the process of privatization the government provided a small fraction of society with ownership rights over previously state owned assets at low prices. The process of privatization was nontransparent and very disputable which made these property rights quite insecure. High tax rates and complexity of the taxation system contributed to the dependence of new owners on their informal relations with the authorities. As the result, privatization intensified significantly the informalization of post-Soviet Russian society.

2.3.2 Post-privatization business-state tax relations

On the one hand, privatization provided disappointing results and contributed to the destitute condition of most firms and concentration of gains among a few winners, which led to great inequality in society[28].

On the other hand, soft-budget constraints provided by the government enabled the survival of firms privatized in the first wave of privatization, especially in the manufacturing sector, but hindered the development of competitive environment. The main provision was tax offsets, the so-called negotiated tax liabilities. It actually made firms insensitive to the tax burden and complexity of the tax system since they could not make decisions themselves in response to taxes. They could only contract customized tax liabilities, getting into debt with the government. For firms in the manufacturing sector it was difficult to go completely underground, so they formed the so

[26]See Lieberman, I., Veimetra, R., 1996.

[27]See Gerxhani, K., 2004, p.275.

[28]Stiglitz, J., 2003, p.133-166.

called virtual economy[29]. The mechanism of agreed tax payments inevitably aggravated corruption in the tax organs.

Newly organized firms especially in retail and service sector immediately went underground where they were able to generate unregistered cash to cover their current costs. The Russian specific is that unregistered cash became a practice not of self-employed, but small and middle enterprises and fly-by-night firms[30]. A great number of "fly-by-night" firms, through which huge amounts of taxes are evaded, appear as a result of the inefficient system of enterprises state registration. It is interesting to note, that according to the survey made by Yakovlev (2001), tax authorities did not react to this evading practice, since they should only provide the planned amount of tax revenues and did not want to incur the high costs of tracing firms operating in the shadow economy. Thus, for the majority of economic subjects the costs of engaging in tax evasion were much lower than the possible benefits due to the very small concealment costs, the low probability of detection by tax officials and no corruption costs incurred[31].

The companies in the natural resources sector were the only ones which generated significant cash returns since they possessed the inputs at hand they didn't need to pay for. Physically they were not able to go underground, so the government could rely only on them in order to raise resources to finance government expenditures on key public goods.

Comparing the early (1992-1993) and late (1999-2000) transition period the overall level of tax revenues in GDP dropped from 33.8 to 30.3 percent where the biggest reduction from 9.1 to 5.1 percent of GDP was observed in corporate income taxation[32]. Due to the lack of tax revenues the state could not provide adequate expenditure policies. It failed to redistribute income, although the income taxation was highly progressive. Total expenditures on education, health and social protection account for nearly half of public expenditures, considering that both GDP and the share of public expenditure in GDP are significantly lower than in OECD countries[33]. During the first decade of transition Russia (and CIS countries on the whole) moved away

[29]Where according to Gaddy, C., Ickes, B. (1998) the companies pretended they produced value which was not the case in reality. An enterprise destroys value when the value of inputs purchased from other enterprises exceeds the value of the output that is produced. It occurs fundamentally because of a lack of property rights (or their bad definition), when agents are unable to enforce their rights to income streams. It is this conflict which keeps value destroyers operating (Gaddy, Ickes, p.20).

[30]Under fly-by-night firms we mean the firms which were set up for a short period of time with the purpose to evade taxes.

[31]Yakovlev, A., 2001, p.8.

[32]Mitra, P., Stern, N., 2003, p.46, 48.

[33]ibid., 2003, p.8

from social security contributions-cum-payroll taxation[34]. The firms indicated that the main reason to go underground was the high tax burden of payroll as compared to the social guarantees provided by the state[35].

2.3.3 Lack of social contract and confidence in state institutions

As most of population and the business community[36] did not consider themselves to be profiting from privatization and the economic policy of the government, the state could barely rely on most taxpayers honesty in fulfilling their tax obligations. Consequently, the government was not able to build up a rapport necessary for mutual fiscal responsibility, which has led to a pervasive form of tax evasion. Although the citizens are aware that they do not meet their obligations to the state in some cases (71 percent said, that they fulfilled their obligations in some and most cases), 57 percent of the respondents consider that the state does not fulfill their obligations at all and in most cases[37],[38]. Consequently, tax evasion can be partly seen not as a rational decision-making under uncertainty, but as a response which captures the divergences from this rationality expressed in people's beliefs about the state.

Public opinion polls provide some interesting facts about society's perceptions about tax evasion. Surveys conducted by the Russian Center of Public Opinion's Study (WSIOM) in 2000-2001 showed: among the respondents 60 percent denounce tax evasion by firms and 43 - by private persons, 22 percent understand the companies that evade and 38 - private persons, 11 do not care about the problem and only 2-3 percent of respondents approved tax evasion. In 2000 tax evasion was condemned by 75 percent of respondents. On the whole the attitude to tax evasion can be analyzed as negative although divergencies are taking place. We propose that they may be partly explained by negative perception of the state.

The respondents also find it tolerable when their employers commit evasion by withholding income taxes. Only 38 percent of respondents denounce this form of evasion. Together with the previous argument this result can

[34]The share of social security and payroll taxes in GDP decreased from 9.7 to 8.1 percent between 1992 and 2000.

[35]For further details see Yakovlev, A., 2001.

[36]The numerous part of business community who was not able to participate in the privatization process

[37]See Krasilnikova, M., 2001, p.3.

[38]It is also not confirmed that the society asserts its claims to the state inherited from the Soviet era; the state is rather perceived as adversary.

also be explained by the fact that in Russia there is a small share of economically active population (5-6 percent) who actually can make a decision whether or not to pay taxes and how much to evade based on the standard features of the tax system.

Since firms are the main taxpayers and tax agents through the withholding system and consequently, the main tax evaders, the state tries to reform by reducing their incentives for evasion activities. As firms refer to the high taxation of payroll as the main reason to engage in evasion, the state tried to cut social taxes. These cuts should be mostly offset by increases in other taxes or expenditure reductions due to inflationary pressures associated with fiscal relaxation[39]. The latter is more likely to happen. Consequently, society is worse off in terms of state benefits such as pensions, wages of state employees, education and health system which produces a further negative attitude towards the state. Moreover, corruption and extortion in state institutions, partly induced by the low wages in the public sector, reinforce the lack of confidence in the state.

It is quite a common view in Russian society that relations with the state should be built up rather on individual negotiations than on the rule of law, and they are correspondingly realized.

2.3.4 Tax rates and the complexity of the tax system

This factor is often seen as typical and the most important cause for going underground, although it can only partly explain the high informalization. We consider this factor because by setting up the modern tax system at the beginning of transition the tax burden was unbearably high. The last Russian tax reforms characterized the above aim of reducing the scale of tax evasion to provide better opportunities for business to work legally. As has been mentioned the following measures were introduced: decrease of tax rates (mainly in direct taxation), which leads to the increasing share of indirect taxation in total tax revenues, especially the taxes on oil sector; elimination of tax favors und progressivity of individual income taxation, provision of the withholding system instead of voluntary reporting for the employees.

Reduction of the tax burden on the whole and tax rates in particular is good and can help to bring down evasion. Since in Russia there are also other particular causes of tax evasion, the impact of reduction in tax rates on increasing the tax revenues should be assessed carefully. There are different views regarding the assessment of this impact.

---

[39]Concluding Statement of the IMF Mission to the Russian Federation, Moscow, June 24, 2004.

The business community strongly supports any reduction of taxes. In the 1990's they claimed that high tax rates were the main reason to go underground, now they point at corruption and extortion in the tax collection process. Whether or not firms actually reduced their evasion level remains unclear as they do not report it.

Some interesting facts can again be inferred from Russian society's opinion. Before the introduction of a flat personal income tax rate of 13 percent the respondents were asked to say whether they support or do not support this reform. 53 percent on average of the adult population (55 percent of the working population) didn't support this measure (34 and 37 percent supported, "hard to say" answers were discarded). After the introduction of this rate only 14 percent of the respondents believed it was justifiable [40] which could partly be attributable to the fact of bounded rationality and not to the tax burden. Their perception is influenced by other non-economic reasons such as distrust in the state. As an outcome, 48 percent of the respondents didn't think this measure helped to reduce income concealment and consequently the evasion of income and payroll taxes (29 percent thought it helped)[41]. It can serve as an indirect indication that society considers other reasons rather than high tax rates influence tax evasion in Russia.

The Ministry of Taxation of the Russian Federation reported an increase in tax revenues in 2001 and 2002 for individual income tax[42]. They also pointed out in October 2003 the enlargement of the tax base on unified social tax. The question is whether these new laws will make much of a difference[43]. The International Monetary Fund, on the other hand, recommended that budgets should be based on conservative assumptions about the impact of the reduction in social tax rates on the revenue base[44]. Calls for more optimistic assumptions are not supported by experience from other countries. They propose to offset these tax cuts by increases in other taxes or expenditure reductions. The IMF supports raising oil sector taxation and believes that

[40]The results can be also explained by the fact that the majority of population are low-income earners and are not influenced by the reform whereas they do not want higher income groups will be taxed lightly.

[41]See Krasilnikova, M., 2001.

[42]See Overview: progress of tax reform, Ministry of Taxation of the Russian Federation, October 2003.

[43]States within the state: Russia's institutions seem designed to ensure that nothing changes, The Economist, 19 July 2001.

[44]See Concluding Statement of the IMF Mission to the Russian Federation, Moscow, 24 June, 2004.

excise taxes could be increased[45]. Although high tax rates may cause an increase in tax evasion, their reduction does not obviously decrease it.

Often it is pointed out that the simplicity of taxation leaves little scope for firms to engage in tax evasion. For example, tax favors compel companies to look for any possible ways to minimize their tax obligations. Sometimes tax avoidance is the first step to tax evasion for companies trying to minimize their tax liabilities. The elaboration of more sophisticated schemes results in tax evasion. Tax avoidance is seen as a normal activity in which companies are actively engaged. It is connected with incurrence of more costs that not all firms can afford to avoid. The Russian legal system does not distinguish precisely when it penalizes after auditing. The tax authorities punish fully for all tax dodging. So tax evasion can be seen as more beneficial. The natural resource companies mainly practice tax avoidance since for them it is difficult to be involved in pure underground activities[46].

2.3.5 Inefficient tax enforcement mechanisms and incompetence

The previous sections show that the economic agents are ready to cooperate rather with tax officials as their "contract" partners for improving the welfare of both, than with the state for the presumed public goods which hardly reach them. Therefore the improvement of the Russian tax system is seen not only in reforms of tax laws, but also tax administration which would be able to collect and enforce taxes. Since they often need to provide a fixed amount of tax revenue planned for a certain period, tax authorities have no incentive to be engaged in the high cost enforcement, i.e. tracing non-registered firms or self-employed individuals. On the other hand, they have recently tend to attack firms aggressively to enforce tax collection[47]. Sometimes their claims are not justifiable, producing an overall negative attitude from business and the population. Often, tax officials are not aware of the schemes provided by professional auditors and accountants.

The enforcement mechanism is more connected with administrative rather than tax policy issues, and there is nothing specific about tax administration

[45] Concluding Statement of the IMF Mission to the Russian Federation, Moscow, 24 June, 2004.

[46] In the literature tax evasion and tax avoidance are treated as separate activities where from the economic point of view evasion implies uncertainty by agent's decision-making and avoidance implies certainty on the part of the taxpayer at the time when he makes his decisions (Cowell, F., p.12).

[47] Putin keeps his promise to oligarchs, initiates tax reforms (2005), MosNews, 28.03.2005.

in this concern. It suffers from the same problems as the other state institutions in Russia which are responsible for law enforcement. Corruption and extortion are among the most serious problems.

2.3.6 Corruption

The process of privatization and the consequent results of the reforms amplified corruption at all levels. More discretion at the disposal of the state including tax administration at regional and local levels enhanced the ability of the government officials to extract money for their own purposes, brought about a further indirect effect in creating a more adverse business climate, characterized by highly distortionary taxation imposed on formal sector of the economy.

Experts and people assessed the corruption level as very high[48] which brings additional disincentive for citizens to comply with tax law. Below the ministry of internal affairs and traffic police the tax authorities are ranked just as the most corrupt element of society. Practically all direct and indirect factors that promote corruption can be observed in Russia: regulation, taxation, provision for goods and services at below market prices, financing of parties, quality of the bureaucracy, level of public sector wages, penalty systems, institutional controls, transparency of rules, laws and processes, examples set by the leadership[49].

Mainly firms have frequent contact with the authorities and attempt to establish good relations with the tax administration. Having this relational capital provides incentives and improves the position of both. If the taxpayer knows who can be bribed with certainty, he does not need to care about proper accounting, and the corrupt official can even help to circumvent their tax liabilities. The costs of evasion are minimized. Additional benefits in terms of difference between the evaded taxes and the sum of the bribe are generated. If the tax official trusts in the taxpayer, the probability of being caught is minimized; the costs which the tax official incurs are minimized; he gets the additional payment which, taking into account the low wages in the public sector, increases his benefits considerably. Relational capital can provide the realization of these conditions. Gaddy, C., Ickes, B. (1998) considered relational capital as an enterprises endowment, especially at the beginning of transition. The more tax authorities are ready to be bribed, the more compliance with tax laws declines and the incidence of taxation becomes arbitrary, thus inevitably leading to tax evasion. The corruptibility

[48] According the survey of WSIOM (2001), International Transparency, World Bank. For example, International Transparency ranked Russia as 86 among 113 countries in 2003.

[49] This classification follows Tanzi, V., 2000.

of other state institutions (police, courts) also eases tax evasion. Paying encourages further extortion[50].

Corruption seemed to improve in the early 2000s but has grown as a problem in recent years despite of some reforms undertaken by the Russian government. Today one out of five firms report that it always uses bribes to get things done. Moreover, corruption is not seen as an obstacle for doing business in Russia[51].

Summing up, the following conclusions can be made:

1. Privatization intensified the informalization of post-Soviet Russian society. The privatization process didn't remove the strong link between the state and non-state activities and preserved the importance of social networks. As a result the social contract is based on negotiations rather than on rule of law, including the tax law.

2. High tax rates at the beginning of transition helped to escalate the evasion in the Russian economy. Reduction of tax rates is good and if budgets allow to do so, it may help to bring tax evasion down. But taking into account the other determinants of tax evasion such as lack of confidence in the state and its institutions, the effect of tax rate reduction should be assessed cautiously.

3. The inefficiency of the law enforcement mechanism is pervasive, and the tax authorities are only a part of a complex problem and could not be considered separately. Corruption and extortion in the tax collection process are important causes of tax evasion.

2.4 Mechanisms of tax evasion

The methods of evading taxes are numerous according to the particular taxes being evaded. Since three groups of taxes - taxes on income, profits and capital gains (7.9 percent of GDP), social security and payroll taxes (8.1) and value-added tax (6.5)- comprise the main part of tax revenues of 30.3 percent of GDP[52] in 1999-2000, and are consequently mostly subject to evasion. Since individual income taxes are paid on a withholding basis with social security and payroll taxes, they are correspondingly evaded together by the employer.

[50]Blood money: Corruption in Russia, The Economist, 20 October 2005.

[51]Anderson, J.H., Gray, C.W., 2006, Anticorruption in Transition 3: Who is succeeding... and why? The World Bank.

[52]See, Mitra, P., Stern, N. Tax systems in transition, p.26.

2.4.1 Individual income tax and unified social tax

Comprising the greater proportion of an enterprise's tax payments, which are evaded, income tax of employees and payroll taxes are always under reforms aimed at reducing tax rates and thus legalizing labor income. 13 percent flat tax rate for individual income and further reduction of the unified social tax with the regressive scale to 26 percent for payroll of 300,000 RUR (app. 10,000 USD), 10 percent - for payroll of 300,000-600,000 RUR (app. 10,000-20,000 USD) and 2 percent - for payroll of more than 600,000 RUR (app. 20,000 USD)[53] are seen as the main measures to reduce tax evasion, though many enterprises can hardly use this regressive scale due to the very low wage level.

The main idea to evade these taxes consists of the fictitious substitution of the payroll, which is liable to taxation, by other costs. There is a systematical understating of employees and owners income through the change in the cost structure. The reason for this substitution is, for example, a contract between a taxpayer and a "fly-by-night" company, according to which a taxpayer transfers money to the bank account of a "fly-by-night" company for a fake report on rendered services. The "fly-by-night" firm pays to the taxpayer the transferred money in cash minus charges deducted. This "premium" amounts to 2-3 percent of the initial payment. The taxpayer pays in cash the agreed wages to the employees and income to the owners concealing most of due taxes.

In 2003 the Tax Ministry initiated a procedure of re-registration of firms set up before July 2002, which aimed to bring under control the system of firms state registration. Thus, companies try to minimize their tax liabilities using contracts with insurance firms. According to the tax law, if a company buys insurance for its employees, it does not need to pay a unified social tax. It transfers to an insurance company the employee's wages as insurance payments, thus evading social und payroll taxes. In reality the employer substitutes life insurance, which is not liable to taxation, for wage payments[54].

Top managers and executives of legally working companies prefer to register as individual entrepreneurs, paying instead of 13 percent of their earned income only 6 percent. Exactly this is what incriminated, among other aspects, to Khodorkovsky and Yukos's top-management team.

If a company in retail trade and services is able to receive revenues in cash, it also uses a scheme of wage payment understating. Moreover, it can

[53]Russian Tax Code, Part 2, Chapter 24.

[54]Volvach, D., Shnurov, K. (2004) The insurance schemes of tax evasion: what the experience tells, The Russian Tax Courier 10.

also conceal a part of output, minimizing its liabilities for value-added and profit tax payments.

2.4.2 Indirect taxes (Value-added tax and customs)

The evasion of indirect taxes, mainly of value-added tax, takes the form of output concealment or understatement and occurs essentially in illegal sector of the economy. That is why the size of shadow economy corresponds roughly to the output which is not covered by VAT. The firms, especially in the production sector, which operate legally, also try to minimize their VAT obligations. They transfer part of the VAT burden to the fly-by-night intermediate trading firms. For example, a firm which produces IT services and products is able to reimburse the whole sum of VAT if it sells their products to a trading firm which will disappear in the nearest future.

Certain problems are observed in taxation of external economic activity. The most important one is VAT reimbursement to exporting companies, applying 0 percent tax rate[55]. Honest exporters suffer since the amount of evasion by the illegitimate VAT reimbursement is big and tax authorities create additional barriers to prevent it. For illegitimate VAT reimbursement fly-by-night companies are also used, which are liquidated as soon as they receive the VAT from exporters not paying the due taxes to the budget. At the same time, exporters have a legal right to reimbursement of taxes paid to their suppliers.

Some other schemes such as false export or setting the production costs too high are also applied[56]. Such schemes are used in import and domestic transactions as well. False export (re-import) is seen to be the most acute problem of the VAT-evasion. In some cases companies can export goods and services and then, misusing the weaknesses of customs and border officials inclined to corruption, re-import these products. In this case the taxpayer is able to claim VAT reimbursement for exported goods and services and to evade import VAT and customs payments by bribing officials or selling products to the underground economy. Sometimes goods do not leave the country, thus reducing the problem of evasion to the quick VAT reimbursement.

Some export associations set up an intermediate company, which buys goods from the producer, pays VAT, then exports claiming VAT reimbursement. The producer (as a rule, a big plant) is one in tax arrears, including VAT. An intermediate or an affiliated company can also make domestic transactions leading to tax liabilities but ceases its activity before paying taxes to

[55] Antel, S. Changes to the tax system, International Tax Review, October 2003.

[56] For further details see Panskov, V., 2003, p.202.

the budget, keeping the whole sum of the contract and VAT. Certainty the fly-by-night firms do not function independently, but are closely connected with a number of intermediaries. Every link in this chain could be potentially used as a "money-laundering" company for illegal non-payment of 20 percent of the turnover on every stage [57]. This high "risk premium" allows taxpayers not only to cover respective costs, but gives them considerable competitive advantages.

The distortions of competition caused by evasion compel other taxpayers to practice avoidance through "holding" schemes with or without the "operating company", capital flight in off-shore or other zones of preferential taxation. The scale of evasion from VAT is illustrated by the fact, that only 41 percent of GDP is taxed by value added tax. The mechanism of special accounts is seen to be a solution to make the settlements more transparent. They should accumulate all "input" and "output" VAT, the difference of which is paid to the budget; the VAT reimbursement ("input" VAT) goes automatically to the analogous special accounts of suppliers. Banks are considered to be responsible for the control of the special accounts regime, but it can be problematic in practice, since banks are closely connected with the companies in implementing their mutually beneficial "optimization" strategies. Some economists propose as a tax base the added value itself for companies calculating it on their own[58].

Another problem in taxation of external economic activity is connected with its complicated regulations by the norms of tax, customs and budget laws, which contradict each other. It creates additional incentives for taxpayers to evade using all possible favors provided for regulation of external economic activity: preferential tax and customs rates, customs regimes. Since the total customs examination of consumer goods, which form 47 percent of Russian imports can not be implemented, taxpayers pay customs according to the lowest rates. Approximately 95 percent of consumer goods' turnover is composed of goods with low import duties' rates understated by the taxpayers. It seems expedient to establish legally a unified approach to customs registration of consumer goods with a unified customs value and rate.

The problem of misuse of customs favors also brings about some tax evading strategies and distortions of competition. Thus more than one third of all favors for payments of customs fall on favors for medicines and other medical goods. But these favors reach neither medical institutions nor people, since the law does not provide direct delivery allowing intermediaries to use

---

[57] The VAT rate has been recently reduced till 18 percent; the further reductions are planned.

[58] For further details see Panskov, V. Russian system of taxation: problems of development, 2003, p.208.

the favors. Sale price could thus be 2.5 times higher than purchase price. Special economic zones, for example, Kaliningrad, serve as places for export and import without customs and quantity restrictions, stimulating evasion. The functioning of such zones does not contradict federal laws, but produces substantial losses to regional and local budgets. The tax favors are provided to taxpayers at the expense of the territories, where tax bases are actually formed. Furthermore, deductions on the social and economic development of special economic zones are not adequate to the amount of tax advantages provided.

The government also grants favors, in addition to those provided by the tax law, within the scope of some commercial projects. This allows participants to reduce the costs of a project's realization; the financial participation of the state amounts to decrease of the projects' costs and the total volume of investments at the federal budget's expense. In such cases the state should be compensated by increasing its share in the capital of these corporations.

2.4.3 Profit tax

Profit taxes are the other part of the majority of evaded tax payments. The reduction of corporate statuary rate from 35 to 24 percent also aims to rapidly bring most enterprises out of the underground economy. To compensate for the reduction, capital investment allowance, which was actively used by industrial firms, was abolished. Furthermore, the tax base was reduced by eliminating the previous restrictive list of deductible business expenses and replacing it with a principle of all necessary and supportable expenses being deductible[59].

Profit understatement and submission of zero bottom accounts are also widely practiced by companies operating legally. They try to use every possibility for increase in costs, except labor costs. Transfer pricing is the most widely accepted form of profit minimization between dependent companies. Since it is practically impossible to determine the market price for many goods, for example, produced abroad or with unique characteristics, realization of the arm's length principle is very difficult to achieve.

The lack of domestic oil market allows oil companies to minimize their tax payments using transfer pricing[60], zones of preferential taxation, creating different organizational structures, money flows and calculations schemes. Since there are no market prices for oil, an additional 2-4 bln.USD of potential tax payments remain with the oil companies through the use of "legal"

[59] See Antel, S. Changes to the tax system, The International Tax Review, October 2003 and the Russian Tax Code, Part 2, Chapter 25.

[60] NEWSru.com, 26.01.2004.

schemes instead of being paid to the budget. For example, the giant Russian oil company "Sibneft" set up in 2001-2002 a number of formally independent small companies with 5-8 employees, registered in zones of preferential taxation. They were buying the total volume of oil from subsidiaries of "Sibneft" and were reselling it to "Sibneft" itself thus accumulating the profit of the company without performing any functional operations. The whole production process was implemented by "Sibneft"[61],[62].

The Federal Tax Service has recently reported about 2 bln.USD of potential profit tax payments of oil companies lost for the Russian budget in 2004 through off-shores[63]. The problem of oil companies' profit tax evasion remains to be very acute for Russia.

Therefore it would be more optimal to tax extractive industries using the appropriate taxation of rents, thus limiting opportunities for minimization at the stages of production, sale and export. Minimization of profit tax is possible by using some tax favors. Thus companies transferring money for charitable purposes can deduct these expenses from taxable profit. After transfers are made, investors get a part of them (from 15 to 75 percent) back in cash.

We make the following conclusions:

1. Individual income tax on withholding basis, unified social tax, profit tax, value-added tax and custom duties if the firm is engaged in external economic activity are the most evaded taxes in Russia. Tax evasion is mainly widespread among firms.

2. Evasion is executed through the understatement of payroll, output and overstatement of other costs (including the non-incurred costs) to bring the profits possibly to zero.

3. The different methods of evasion (through fly-by-night firms, unregistered cash, tax advantages, etc.) are mainly based on collusions with other companies, banks and state officials.

2.5 Recent proposals for improvement

The critical situation of the pervasive evading activities of firms was one of the main reasons to carry out recent tax reforms. Consequently, firms were

[61]See Panskov, V., 2003, p.177

[62]The government also impedes the creation of domestic oil market forcing the oil companies to set favorable domestic oil prices in order to slow inflation down.

[63]See the Interfax's website for further details (www.interfax.ru/e/B/0/0.html?id issue=11428564).

expected to begin operating legally and to increase their due tax payments as a reaction to the tax rates reduction, that on the whole would speed up growth of the economy. The budget losses from this reduction would be thus easily recovered. The analysis of the reforms will give insights as to whether the considerable reduction of tax rates is a good policy instrument for combating tax evasion. The Russian reality gives some preliminary results on this issue.

The tax authorities consider as a great success the reduction of *payroll taxes*, since they report increase of the tax base for individual income tax and the social unified tax. This tax base broadening is mainly explained by the increase of wages. The fact is quite explainable from the point of view of economic theory: labor bears the burden of payroll taxes[64].

Ivanova, A., Keen, M. and Klemm, A. analyzed the Russian flat tax reform and came to the conclusion that the reform itself didn't cause the revenue boom of personal income taxes[65]. The empirical study conducted by Vasiljeva, A. et.al (2004) estimated the contribution of different factors to the observed increase of individual income tax and a less than might be expected decrease of unified social tax, after the reform in 2001, in percentage of GDP. The results are summarized in table 2.2.

As can be inferred from table 2.2, budget losses of 1.8 percent GDP from the reduction of tax rates were compensated only by 0.3 percent by the increase in legally declared wages. The small effect of the reduction of individual income tax can be also explained by the fact that approximately 90 percent of taxpayers paid income tax according to the minimum tax rate before the reform.

The reduction of *profit tax* has led to a considerable decrease of revenues from this tax. The budget losses are estimated at 1.42 percent of GDP. Direct effects are among the main factors of these losses (decrease of the nominal tax rate as well as elimination of tax favors). The latter effect and especially the abolition of investment credit contributed to the further increase of tax evasion of profit tax. This measure does not improve the investment process in the Russian economy.

Elimination of turnover taxes was not directly intended to reduce the evasion level of the economy, but contributed to the reduction of tax burden in industry and to the simplification of the tax system.

Some economists (Gurvich, Vasiljeva) suggest not to reduce but rather redistribute the tax burden. The availability of rich natural resources with wide export orientation makes shifting the tax burden to the extracting in-

[64]See Rosen, H., 2002, p.265

[65]See Ivanova, A. et al., 2005, p.40.

dustry very attractive and quite reasonable. The introduction of tax on mineral extraction was estimated as a positive measure in this direction.

Table 2.2: Factors' contribution to the tax compliance after the reform of income tax (as percentage of GDP)

		Contributed by					
				indirect effect of the reform of			
Taxes	Total effect	decrease of the tax rate	exiting the shadow economy	unified social tax	turnover taxes	economic cycle of the labor market	other effects
Unified social tax	-0.6	-1.7	0.2	0.4	0.1	0.3	0
Income tax	0.4	-0.1	0.1	0.1	0.1	0.1	0.2
Total	0.2	-1.8	0.3	0.5	0.2	0.4	0.2

Source: Vasiljeva, A., Gurvich, E. (2004) The structure of the Russian tax system, Research Paper, Expert economic group, p.9.

The tax as well as export duty is constantly reconsidered according to the world oil prices and in August 2005 amounted to 2,273 RUR (approximately 66 EURO) for one ton[66]. With the export duty it is possible to collect up to 100 percent of the pure profits of the oil companies.

The oil companies point out at the arbitrary (since levied ad valorem) and distortionary (since they duplicate each other) character of these two taxes. The concept of taxation of natural resource rents in terms of income from

[66]Ministry of Taxation of the Russian Federation, August 2005.

natural resource use seems to be more justifiable, but there are no practical mechanisms for its realization in the tax system.

Since the above-mentioned problems of Russian taxation and the evading strategies are very difficult to control and handle, some Russian economists (Vasin, A.) pay attention to investigation of the special tax regimes as presumptive policy options for Russian tax structures. As taxation of rents from natural resource may be a solution for big enterprises, because of its considerable resource-orientation, the united tax on imputed (normative) income for some kinds of activity and the simplified system of taxation are considered to be appropriate for small businesses.

Small and medium sized enterprises do not play an important role in the economy and in the forming of all level budget revenues. From small businesses the budget system receives less than 1 percent of the consolidated budget revenues. Approximately 5 million taxpayers are reckoned as those to be taxed as small enterprises. But the half of them are engaged in entrepreneurial activity without registration with the tax organs or without submission of any information to the statistical and tax authorities, or just submitting so-called zero bottom line accounts[67].

The simplified system considers the payment of one tax on gross income (6 percent) or profit (15 percent) instead of paying profit tax, property tax and unified social tax. Organizations which apply the system are also released from VAT. Consequently, their buyers can not get the reimbursement of "input" VAT[68]. This measure of VAT release is often seen as insignificant. Companies do not regard indirect taxes as a particular burden, because they aim to pass them on to consumers. In case of the simplified system VAT payment will help to solve the problem of its reimbursement.

To the end of 2002 only 50,000 organizations and 100,000 individual entrepreneurs have been applying the simplified system, mainly in retail trade and services for cash. This can be explained by the restrictions concerning annual gross income (15 millions RUR or app. 430,000 EURO) and value of basic funds (100 millions RUR or app. 3 million EURO)[69]. These rules exclude many industrial firms from using the system. Furthermore, under the general trend of the total tax favors abolition, small enterprises were deprived of the profit tax's favor, which was used mainly by industrial firms. However, the simplified system is actively used by individual entrepreneurs, which allows them to reduce their tax liabilities from 13 to 6 percent of the taxable income. Since the restriction on annual gross income is not applied for indi-

[67]See Panskov, V., 2003, p.113.

[68]See the Russian Tax Code, Part 2, Chapter 26.

[69]See Antol, S., 2003.

vidual entrepreneurs, the scheme is widely used by top managers of Russian big companies. Meanwhile, the simplified system of taxation is considered as a crucial part of small business's taxation, which will allow legalizing its activity.

The united tax on imputed (potential) income for some kinds of activity (retail trade and services) aims mainly to remove cash circulation from the shadow sphere. According to different estimates, 30 to 80 percent of registered goods and services provided by small and medium-sized enterprises are sold for cash. In the beginning of 2003, cash comprised 36 percent of all money volume in the economy (in developed countries not more than 7-9 percent). Taking into account the lack of state control, this contributes to money transfers into the shadow economy thus guaranteeing tax evasion. Control on the part of commercial banks is also not implemented. Meanwhile, banks provide, for example, individual entrepreneurs with cash, which makes up 70 percent in the structure of banks' cash turnover. Expert estimates show that approximately 40 percent of retail trade is not covered by taxes[70].

The dependence of taxpayers on subjectivism of tax organs should be reduced with the application of united tax on imputed income - one of the main questions related to corruption and extortion in tax administration. A large part of unpaid taxes goes into the pockets of corrupt bureaucrats at different levels.

But taxation of normative income is a more complicated issue than it appears to be. Thus some problems have arisen with the introduction and payment of this tax. Regional authorities determined the basic profitabitity without any economic grounds. As a result the indices of basic profitability for the same activities differed in different regions (in Novgorod 56 times higher than in Tambov in 2002)[71]. This is connected to the fact that federal authorities did not provide united methodology for estimation of small business activity. Companies determine their structures under different uncertain factors. Particularly in a competitive economic environment, firms face considerable risk factors, such as price fluctuations, which can influence the profit variance. It requires from the government a more complicated approach related to tax calculation depending on the production capacities employed by the firms at any period. In this case corruption can also arise.

The Code considerably reduces the number of potential taxpayers under the united tax on imputed income. On the one hand, this creates a wider platform for the functioning of the shadow economy with income sheltering and tax evasion. On the other hand, the system of taxation, according to

[70] For further details see Panskov, V., 2003, p.225.

[71] ibid., p.115.

which the tax base is determined by the state, not as a result of economic activity, can be considered far from ideal. Such regimes may exist only in a particular economic situation, and can not be seen as a long-term policy objective. This form of taxation seems to be attractive in the presence of tax evasion, since it appears not to be distortionary and allows the government to maximize tax revenues without administrative costs. But in the long run firms can also evade by looking for substitutes for the taxed inputs (the total size of the shop, the number of employees, etc.).

We conclude with the following statements:

1. In order to reverse the situation characterized by the critical evasion level in the economy, the state took the following measures: reduction of tax rates of the most evaded taxes, the abolition of tax favors and simplification of the tax system by reducing the number of taxes and introducing simplified regimes of taxation for some economic agents. The first empirical studies show that these reforms contribute to the improvement of tax compliance only to a small extent.

2. The tax burden on the mining sector, especially on the oil industry in the situation of favorable world prices, was considerably increased and imposed on "administrative assessments". Export duty and the tax on oil extraction are levied ad valorem on weight thus reducing the scope of tax evasion by export.

3. The concept of presumptive taxation has become very popular in this regard, especially those regimes which allow determination of the due taxes according to the observable characteristics of taxpayers. The main idea is to take advantage of data that is easier for officials to obtain on the one hand, and to reduce the scope of discretion of the tax authorities on the other.

2.6 Summary

The positive analysis of tax evasion in Russia provides an overview of the tax environment, the scale of the phenomenon, main determinants and mechanisms of tax evasion as well as the recent attempts and proposals to improve tax compliance in the Russian economy. Recent years are characterized by significant reforms in the tax sphere aiming to ease the tax burden of entities which claim high taxes to be the main reason for their evasion.

The studies refer to very different estimates of the shadow economy in Russia, the economy which is not covered by taxes. Since they aim to measure unobservable activity, the estimations differ according to the chosen explanatory variables. Consequently, the main value of the empirical studies is to figure out which factors cause tax evasion in a particular country. In international comparison, Russia, like other transition economies, is characterized by the level of the shadow economy between developed and developing countries, namely between 30 and 50 percent of GDP according to different authors. So there are explicit country distinctions in the informalization of the economy.

The stable level of tax evasion in Russia is characterized by the following consequent determinants: privatization mechanisms, tax relations of business to the state, lack of social contract and confidence in state institutions or rather a social contract based on individual negotiations rather than on rule of law - law enforcement mechanism including a tax administration prone to corruption and extortion, the tax system.

Since the tax system provides opportunities for tax evasion, it is tax reform which intended to reduce incentives to engage in evading activities. But the tax system can not be considered in isolation from other underlying determinants of tax evasion. They are often ignored as those which have no consequences for the development of tax evasion. Meanwhile, the privatization process which failed to separate state from non-state activities, the social contract with the state based on individual negotiations and relations rather than on rule of law, induced corruptive and extortive behavior have complementary explaining power of the phenomenon of tax evasion in Russia.

Such issues as social norms, cooperative behavior, and functioning of institutions, have their impact on the development of tax evasion.

The mechanisms of tax evasion are rather simple and aim to understate some economic indices such as output, profit and payroll and overstate other costs. The entities manage to implement them by colluding with other companies, banks and state officials, creating fictitious (fly-by-night) firms, using operations with cash, etc. As a result of recent tax reforms, tax rates on the most evaded taxes were considerably reduced in order to bring evasion down, tax favors were abolished in order to broaden tax bases, the number of taxes, especially those which had been imposed by regional and local authorities were also decreased. In spite of some positive steps, significant reduction of evasion is not observed; evasion of profit tax has even increased.

Simplified tax regimes and presumptive taxation are also seen as attractive instruments to reduce the level of tax evasion: the first one is designed for small businesses and very favorable for them, the second one is intended for particular activities where cash circulation is especially high. In the situation of the much liberalized "normal" tax system, the existence of the simplified tax regime seems to be not necessary: in case of pervasive evasion in the economy it can serve as an escape from the "normal" system. It is also not proven that the level of evasion among small firms has decreased due to this regime[72].

Taxation based on observable characteristics of taxpayers and not on economic results also appears appropriate to bring evasion down, since tax authorities can easily verify the due taxes with less scope for corruption or extortion. The presumptive assessment is used today for the taxation of export oil. Export duty and tax on oil extraction are levied ad valorem for a ton. Due to these taxes the tax burden on exported oil and pressure on the oil companies through the tax system have considerably increased. It also reflects the position of some economists who propose to tax rents from natural resources more heavily thus shifting the tax burden to the mining sector. Thereby diversification of the economy would be increased.

Positive analysis of tax evasion in Russia allows us to distinguish two types of problems: direct tax policy issues and indirect country-specific features which influence the level of evasion in the economy. Consequently, there is a need to consider two types of theoretical contributions to the tax evasion problem: taxation theory and the public choice theory of tax evasion.

[72]Such regimes are very applicable in the developing countries (for more on this issue see Bird R., Wallace, S. (2003), Is it really so hard to tax the hard-to-tax? ITP Paper 0307). But the authors concluded that such regimes do not seem to help combating evasion in these countries. Moreover, the high educational level in Russia allows compliance with the "normal" tax system.

Chapter 3

The normative analysis of tax evasion

The determinants and mechanisms of tax evasion of firms imply rather comprehensive modelling of many economic incentives to be able to make any reasonable policy implications. Firms are more prone to the whole range of economic incentives which can influence their behavior regarding evasion. Apart from the impact of tax system and the enforcement mechanism on the individual decision making about tax evasion, there is also an overall impact created by the social, institutional and procedural features of the whole economic system. These are the aspects through which differences in evasion level of countries can be explained, so that country-specific mechanisms of creating particular incentives should be considered.

3.1 Privatization aspects in the theoretical context

Sappington and Stiglitz (1987) were the first who pointed out that privatization is associated with transaction costs when the government tries to intervene into firm's activity. These costs are generally higher under private ownership than under public ownership. Analogous to the Fundamental Theorem of Welfare Economics, the authors present the fundamental privatization theorem which sets the conditions under which private production is Pareto-efficient, and the reasons why privatization may not achieve the most desired outcome are considered, so-called "privatization failures". The privatization is claimed to achieve efficiency if it is accomplished through the following auction: the state auctions the right to produce among the bidders with symmetric beliefs about costs the payment equal to the government's valuation of output. The state primarily "compensates" the producer who presents the highest bid according to its valuation of output (it guarantees that the state reports the true valuation level). The producer then produces the efficient amount of output corresponding to the government valuation and gives "the compensation" back to the government. Among the reasons why these ideal conditions can not be fulfilled are, the possibility of the private owner to earn rents, which occur, for example, due to the limited competition at the bidding stage; the institutional restrictions on contracts and costs; the problems of contracts' implementation, which include among others the difficulties to measure the performance of the private owner. In this regard, when the transaction costs of future government interventions and influences are expected to be high, privatization most likely leads to inefficiencies.

In case of Russian privatization issues the implication of the Coase Theorem was more frequently considered[1]. It was argued that once property rights were established, no matter how, efficient outcome would be provided. The new owners would require the establishment and support of necessary institutions of the state. As we see, it definitely did not happen in Russia. This is why privatization exacerbated the specific relations of private enterprises with the state, where the state could not provide public goods necessary to manage private property efficiently. Consequently, private enterprises did not want or could not pay taxes and preferred to evade.

The model of Boycko, Shleifer and Vishny (1996) emanates from the commonly shared opinion that public enterprises perform poorly and efficiency improves after privatization and subsequently proves it. Since in the model privatization means the assignment of control rights over employment from the politicians to the manager, the critical parameter here is who controls labor spending. If the politician exercises this control he chooses, as it is assumed by the model, the inefficiently higher amount of labor spending. They employ the objective function of the politician as a difference between the potential political benefit resulted from excess employment and political costs of the profits foregone by the state from such excessive labor spending. The objective function of the manager is simply given by his share of profits. In this case partial ownership of both the state and the private owner is considered. The manager can bribe the politician to change his decision from the higher labor spending. If their combined utility will be higher at a lower labor spending, the bribe is efficient. With corruption they can choose the outcome, which will be efficient for both from their joint point of

[1]See Coase, R.H. (1960) The Problem of Social Cost, Journal of Law and Economics, October.

view. Though the corruption can raise efficiency since the private owner by the bribe can reduce inefficiency, society does not improve and it leads not always to the first best.

When privatization occurs, the share of managers in the firm increases and they get control rights. In order to maximize profits they choose the efficient level of labor spending. But the politician can try to maximize the political support aiming at excessive employment by subsidizing the firm. The model proves that with control rights the managers choose efficient labor spending and restructuring even when they must forego subsidies from the state. The objective functions of the politician and the manager are modified when the function of the former is diminished by the cost of making a subsidy to the firm and the function of the latter is increased by the effective subsidy. Without the subsidy it is optimal for the firm to choose efficient labor spending. With the government transfer the firm can choose higher labor spending if it is better off with this amount of spending plus subsidy than with the efficient level of labor spending. The subsidy increases the cost for the politician which can be higher after privatization than the political benefit from excessive employment. In this case privatization leads to restructuring.

Comparing three cases without privatization, without privatization but with corruption and with privatization, the most probable condition in which the restructuring will take place is with corruption. When comparing the situations before and after privatization, in the latter case the politician has to compensate the manager for foregone profits due to excessive employment. The increase of subsidy costs means in the model the realization of a tough monetary policy, which in turn reinforces the working mechanisms of privatization. Not having been able to subsidize destitute firms, in Russia the state allowed tax arrears.

Boycko, Shleifer and Vishny emphasized this point considering privatization in Russia. The important result which can be employed for further analysis is that privatization can be effective if the interests of shareholders (profit maximization) are far away from the interests of politicians (excess employment)[2].

For example, Rosefielde (1998) - examining Russia's situation - explored the idea that the government is very much dependent on support from various interest groups. Ultimately the objective of a politician is to be re-elected and to remain in power, which is not necessarily expressed in maintaining a higher level of employment, at least in Russia. As we could see in the last years in Russia, a politician is able to realize his objectives not caring much

[2]See Boycko, M., Shleifer, A., Vishny, R., 1996, p.316.

about employment. Consequently, political systems and their enforcement mechanisms matter and affect interactions between agents, such as government, taxpayers, and tax authorities.

The second point emphasized that the strategy of creating industrial holding companies as core investors in privatized firms was designed to increase political influence on firms, to achieve the objective of a politician of being re-elected. Boycko, Shleifer and Vishny also point out that a politician can exert control over politicized shareholders in the form of pressure or/and corruption, which can lead to efficient solution for both, saying at the same time that there are some problems with using such methods of enforcement[3].

Earlier papers on privatization (Schmidt (1990), Shapiro and Willig (1990)) underline the role of information in privatization. If a politician has less information about the firm, privatization will be more effective, since it would be easier for the shareholder to gain control rights over the firm. The separation of a politician from the shareholder in the model of Boycko, Shleifer and Vishny goes not through the lack of information between the two, but through the change in the cost-benefit mechanism of a politician, who has to pay more for the maintenance of his objectives. But privatization does not necessarily work under this mechanism. Even if the politician uses subsidies to maintain the higher level of employment in privatized firms, he still can make them costless to himself, as was done in Russia through tax arrears. Since in Russia only big natural resource companies are able to create value, they provide the government with necessary tax revenues, and also support executive and legislative powers in election. It is easier for the government to rely on them to realize its objective function, than on voters, who are not even the main taxpayers in the economy. Privatizing these resource companies and contracting with them by providing a certain amount of tax revenues and election support was the mechanism which exacerbated tax evasion in Russia, where it takes now its pervasive form.

Ahrend and Winograd (2002) investigated the connection between tax evasion and privatization. They employed the political economy model of imperfect taxation. They have modelled imperfect taxation by allowing for fix costs of taxing an individual. This assumption says that if the costs of inspection are above the expected tax payment it is not worthwhile to monitor such a taxpayer, so he completely evades taxes. In the economy with rich, middle-class and poor groups of individuals (where the poor earn no income on their physical or human capital liable to tax) three corresponding situations are considered. In "Low-Income Country" the cost of inspecting of any individual is higher than the expected tax payments no matter what the

[3]Boycko, M., Shleifer, A., Vishny, R., 1996, p.313.

tax rate is. The taxpayers are not monitored and, consequently, do not pay taxes. The extremely poor African countries can resemble this modelling. In "Middle-Income Country", to which the large number of developing and transition economies belongs, it is worthwhile only to tax rich, since the costs to monitor them are less than the expected tax revenues. "High-Income Country" is characterized by the taxation of the rich and the middle-class.

The taxpayers vote for the tax rate which maximizes their personal utilities. The tax rates in voting equilibrium are determined according to the electoral process. In the low income country there will be no taxation as nobody will be profitably taxed. The middle income country will be characterized by taxation of the rich at the highest possible level, since middle and poor are not taxed, but prefer transfers. In the high-income country the situation depends on the income of the middle-class: if it will be below the mean, the middle class will want transfers with the poor as in the previous case and vote for maximum taxation, but if the income is above the mean, the middle-class will want to escape taxes, which means reduction of taxes to the detriment of the poor. In the following the impact of taxation on the privatization outcome is analyzed. After voting on the tax rate there is a decision on privatization, where the efficiency of the tax system is taken as given. The authors differentiate between corrupt and non-corrupt privatization: in the first case the price of a sold asset is below the net present value of future income streams obtained by the government from this asset; in the second case the price is equal or less the NPV of future income obtained by the private owners.

We will describe the main results obtained for the middle-income economy, since Russia obviously belongs to this group. As it is only worthwhile to tax the rich in the middle-income country, the poor favor privatization to the rich since it increases their transfers even at cut down prices. The middle class also wants any form of privatization even knowing that they will not get control over assets, since it also increases their transfers. Consequently, there is a tendency to privatize to the rich in the country with imperfect taxation. Additionally, the authors assume that even with monitoring there is an opportunity for the taxpayer to evade some part of the due taxes through corruption, which changes the willingness to privatize. Due to tax evasion the poor and middle-class get fewer transfers, and thus a tendency of popular support of privatization from the losers diminishes. The result of "political evasion" - the evasion by more powerful and better connected individuals and companies - which in the model are assumed to be practiced only by the rich, does not change the result for the middle-income country. The model thus shows how inefficient taxation characterized by weak tax enforcement and tax evasion through corruption reverse the privatization support from society due to the inability to compensate the losers of the privatization process.

Hoff and Stiglitz (2002) show the stability of such a situation, where the winners of the privatization process may fail to demand the rule of law even if it is the Pareto-efficient "rule of the game". Under the rule of law they understand the environment where the ability of the local, regional, and national authorities to take arbitrary actions is restricted. In Russia, privatization expanded the discretion of authorities. Stripping assets rather than building the value of the firm reflected the situation in Russia after the privatization process. As long as state assets to be distributed exist, those who have the chance to obtain them will try to prolong the no-rule-of-law regime. Further uncertainty about whether the rule of law will be established can lead individuals to choose actions which can adversely affect others (for example, stripping the assets of the privatized firm rather than building its value, tax evasion) and give them an interest in prolonging the no-rule-of-law state.

The political environment characterized as a public good is in the initial state without the rule of law. The authors define the so called switch line - the threshold of realized additional returns below which the value of the firm is built and the rule of law is demanded (since the agents are strictly better off by building value with the rule of law) and above which they strip assets.

Equilibrium is characterized by the stripping ability curve - the fraction of population who strip assets and does not support the rule of law. The intersection of the switch line and the stripping ability curve characterize the interior equilibria. The existence of multiple equilibria is explained by the sufficiently large externality mediated through the political environment. So even if in the equilibrium the fraction of the population who does not support the rule of law equals zero (for everybody it is preferable to build value under the rule of law than to strip assets), the switch line can be steeper than the stripping ability curve at the efficient equilibrium, and further the switch line can cut the stripping ability curve from above. As it happens at the higher fraction of those who do not support the rule of law, a bad equilibrium appears which occurs at the lower switch point lowering the return of the marginal asset-stripper. Consequently, there is a movement away from the efficient to the bad equilibrium. So stripping assets can be also rational. Since it is assumed that the increase of those who do not support the rule of law has a negative impact on the probability of the establishment of the rule of law, transition to the rule of law in the future period will likely not occur. The authors show that such factors as initial conditions, social norms and policy influence the demand for the rule of law. Such Russian features as the existence of assets which are easy to strip (natural resources), diminishing of the importance of social norms and the nature of the privatization process, decrease the political constituency for the rule of law.

Gordon, Bai, Li (1999) made an additional point concerning the fact why privatization can fail in achieving efficiency as happened in Russia. Since, for example, taxes can distort private incentives, high effective tax rates can make private ownership less preferable on efficiency grounds. They prove the trade-off between tax distortions and government control by the example of a trade-off between a volunteer army and draft. Beginning the situation with a small military on a volunteer basis and assuming further increase if its size requires larger and larger increase of the tax rate needed to finance military and non-military expenditures. This increase is necessary because wages in the military should be increased in order to attract more volunteers and there is also an observed decrease of the tax base since more individuals drop out of the labor force. So a very large military would not be attainable since the tax revenues generated at the top of the Laffer-curve would not be enough to finance it. So draft will be more efficient if it is needed to maintain a large army.

Rapid privatization in Russia was aimed at reducing substantially all distortions to market incentives, which in reality did not happen. High implicit tax rates due to the arbitrary behavior of state officials contributed to inefficiency of privatization. The considered models partly explain the incentives which the privatization process in Russia exacerbated and how tax evasion develops in the economic environment thereafter.

The following conclusions can be made:

1. Inefficient privatization can be explained by the high transaction costs of future government interventions and influences. After state assets were privatized in the no-rule-of-law situation the politician could exert control and influence over politicized shareholders. The owners thus follow economic strategies which influence their political position and are not interested in the further establishment of the rule-of-law.

2. Insider privatization at cut down prices, the availability of rich natural resources which are easy to strip, and as a consequence the declined importance of social norms, contribute to the prolonging of the no-rule-of-law situation.

3. High implicit tax rates also induced by the pressure to pay bribes to state officials can distort private incentives making state ownership more efficient.

4. The rational response is tax evasion. Due to this transfers to the rest of society diminish, and there is an observed tendency of declined support for privatization from the losers.

3.2 The theory of tax evasion

3.2.1 Individual income tax and unified social tax

The classics of formal analysis of tax evasion go back to Allingham and Sandmo (1972) and Yitzhaki (1974), who were concerned with the decision of a rational taxpayer whether to evade or not to evade. The decision is taken under risk of being caught, where in the good state of the world the taxpayer keeps the money, he or she does not pay. It can also be interpreted as the benefit derived from the tax evasion. In the bad state of the world the taxpayer is punished with fines, whatever they are (normally they are proportional to evaded tax and considerably exceed the original tax due), measuring his or her income loss and are interpreted as the cost of tax evasion. For the rational taxpayer to undertake tax evasion the benefit should exceed the cost thus raising his or her expected income. In equilibrium the evader thus conceals part of his or her income, taking into account that his or her utility is increased with income and the expected rate of return is positive.

The analysis gives important implications for the structure of tax-enforcement parameters: the probability of detection, the fine parameter and the tax rate. Stricter controls and more fines increase the declared income thus reducing evasion. Increase of the tax rate can lead to the reduction of tax evasion, as well as to its increase depending on the extensions of the basic theoretical model. Introducing to the analysis the measure of risk aversion suggests that if absolute risk aversion decreases as income increases, higher tax rates will lead to greater income declarations and a reduction in evasion[4]. Reduction of disposable income reduces evasion via wealth effect. Consequently, increase in income implies more tax evasion also through pure income effect. The result with an increase of the tax rate holds no more if tax increases imply a concomitant increase in public goods. In this case, perceived total income (private disposable income plus public goods) rises if public goods are underprovided leading to increased tax evasion. If public goods are overprovided a taxpayer perceives a fall in total income, which implies reduced evasion[5].

This primary analysis has limitations. In addition to different income and consumption levels of taxpayers, the system of penalties may be highly uncertain, the probability of being caught is also unknown to a taxpayer. Furthermore, social costs of evasion may be low or even negative reflecting, for example, the unpopularity of the government[6].

---

[4]See Myles, G., 1995, p.387.

[5]See Cowell, F., 1990, p.68.

[6]See Tanzi, V., 2000, p. 174 175.

Since this research is mainly concerned with the tax evasion of enterprises, this basic modelling can be employed by considering the behavior of firms facing the decision under risk. As we have already pointed out it is more appropriate for Russia, where the most part of individual income is taxed on withholding basis, thus releasing taxpayers from filling income tax returns. But companies often substitute for their employees in underreporting wages, at the same time minimizing payroll taxes.

Yaniv (1988) employed the approach of Allingham and Sandmo using the utility function of an employer, which has net profits as its argument, choosing the level of declared wage payments and employment level under risk. In the presence of profit taxation it is optimal for an enterprise to evade withheld taxes as soon as the tax rate on wage payments to be withheld (marginal gain) is more than on profit or, strictly speaking, more than the sum of penalties if detected and overpaid profit tax if not (expected marginal loss). Then it is immediately to conclude that an increase in the tax-enforcement parameters (probability of detection and fines) decreases incentives for evasion leading to more probable costs.

The central comparative static effect of an increase of withholding taxes on evasion was considered under different penalty structures. Since in Russia fines are calculated according to unpaid taxes multiplied by penalty rate and days of evasion when being detected, this effect can be observed in two relevant states: with the refund of overpaid profit tax due to labor cost understating, and without it. The interesting case will also be without profit taxation which is not far from reality due to the high level of profit tax evasion in Russia. The increase of withholding taxes (we mean here the sum of payroll and individual income taxes) produce two types of effects on the level of declared wage payments: substitution and income effects.

The substitution effect arises because of the change in price of a reported relative to an unreported dollar of wage payments when the profit tax can be refunded upon detection. Due to an increase in withholding tax rates this relative price (or simply marginal gains) increases leading to less declaration of wage payments thus producing a negative effect. When there is no profit tax refund and the penalty upon detection is dependent on unpaid taxes (withholding tax rate multiplied by understated wage payments) the substitution effect disappears, since there is no change in the relative price to be observed. The income effect is associated with the change in net profits in both states of the world due to an increase in taxes to be withheld. This increase increases profits in the state of non-detection, but decreases them in the state of detection under considered penalty structure. Whether a firm is credited for its profit tax overpayments or not, the income effect is unambiguously positive pointing that more wage payments are to be declared in case of an increase of the withholding tax. Thus the total effect to be observed here is ambiguous when the profit tax is refunded and unambiguously positive when it is not. The ambiguous effect on declared wage payments is also to be observed by an increase in profit tax.

So the analysis does not leave us with the predictable conclusion, that high payroll and individual income taxes produce a higher level of evasion, sometimes even leading to more declaration of wage payments.

Now let us consider the effect of tax reform in Russia when progressive taxation with broader self-declaration was replaced by the flat tax rate of individual income tax and reduction of united social tax. It may also help us to answer the main question, whether the implementation of the withholding system can reduce tax evasion. We again employ here the approach of Allingham and Sandmo, who analyzed the decision of an individual tax evader how much of his or her income to declare in the absence of a withholding system. This decision can be compared with that of an employer facing how much of wage payments to declare under the withholding system. Comparing two optimal levels of declaration, it is obtained that in equilibrium the marginal rate of substitution between net incomes earned at both states of the world by an individual tax evader would equal the marginal rate of substitution between net profits earned at both states of the world by a company which declares only part of its wage payments[7].

Yaniv employed the logarithmic form of the individual taxpayer and the company's utility functions and found that in the absence of profit taxation the relation between evaded taxes in absence of the withholding system and evaded taxes in presence of the withholding system would equal the ratio between legally earned net individual income and legally earned net profits. Consequently, the withholding system can help to reduce evasion, if the labor costs in output exceed the profit share in output. Furthermore, reduction of withholding taxes will increase evasion under the penalty scheme where fines are dependent on the withholding tax, until the withholding rate has been sufficiently reduced to eliminate the incentive for non-filing[8].

The second main problem in income tax evasion concerns the income of self-employed, so called individual entrepreneurs. They have more opportunities to earn cash being engaged in retail trade or rendering services and able to conceal all or a large part of their income. The separation of labor supply and tax evasion activities definitely brings some additional results. A higher-wage self-employed person is inclined to conceal more income. A tax or increase in tax rate induce him or her to participate more in a risky activ-

[7]Yaniv, G., 1988, p.200.

[8]ibid., p.201, 203.

ity. The result is in accordance with the standard portfolio choice problem, where an increase in income, for example, shifts the taxpayer's budget constraint outward, and equilibrium occurs at the increasing share of concealed income. On the other hand, as wage increases, the number of hours of work can fall leading to less participation in the black economy.

These effects are observed in Russia by high income citizens, who are registered as self-employed persons, and also can explain the structure of illegal sector consisting primary of small and medium firms organized by self-employed, who are not registered in tax organs.

Cowell (1990) analyzed changes in the following parameters[9]: income earned in the legal sector, wages earned underground, probability of detection and fines. Although many self-employed do not operate in the legal sector at all and it is not so easy to start, the result holds that those who are better off in the legal sector work less in the illegal sector. Higher wages earned underground provide an ambiguous effect on working in the black economy since additional effects appear. Moreover, there are no definite connections between engaging in the illegal sector and personal characteristics (risk aversion, attributes, which define the taxpayer's preferences). More probable and more severe fines can exert both negative and positive effects on engagement in the black economy depending on the curvature of labor supply. If the further increase in income induces to reduce the hours worked underground (the so called backward-bending labor supply), then increase of tax-enforcement parameters is not effective. They can reduce the hours of working underground if, and only if, labor supply rises with an increase in the wage. Also an interesting implication can be observed in changing an income tax schedule. Increase in lump-sum transfer can reduce evasion and an increase in progressivity can reduce it among the poor, but encourage among the rich without any changes in tax-enforcement parameters.

Some conclusions can be drawn from the basic analysis of income tax evasion.

1. It can be employed for analyzing corporate tax evasion, where the utility function of an enterprise has profit as its argument, and partly explain its evading activity. It is always optimal to evade if the rate of return to evasion is positive.

2. The theory and Russian evidence suggest that evasion of payroll taxes is observed even if there is a withholding system at source since companies are understating payroll at masse.

[9]See Cowell, F., 1990, p.88-89.

3. According to the theoretical model tax evasion can be reduced with the help of withholding system if the share of labor costs in output would be higher than the profit share in output.

4. The result of tax rate increase has on the whole an indeterminate impact on tax evasion as far as individual income and payroll taxes are concerned.

5. Increase of tax-enforcement parameters (probability of detection and fines) usually reduces the level of tax evasion[10].

The main policy prescription implicit in the basic model is that in order to curb evasion audits have to be stepped out and fines increased[11]. The realization of this kind of enforcement presumes expropriation of all the taxpayer's wealth as the optimal penalty. But enforcement policy is more than these two instruments (probability of audits and fines), for which further considerations in the subsequent subchapters are needed. Given the basic insights, the model sheds light only on the determinants of tax evasion connected with the magnitude of tax rates and tax enforcement parameters ignoring such aspects as the nature of taxpayer's motivation, the importance of interactions and the behavior of firms in the productive economy. We will firstly explore the last area.

3.2.2 Sales taxes

Understating labor costs which allows companies to evade social security payments is only one form of firm's evading activities, when they make false declarations about input use. Companies can also overstate other costs minimizing their obligations for value-added tax. Misreporting sales and profit is another form of evading strategies. Understating revenues minimizes value-added tax's payments; non-declared profits reduce due profit taxes. Since profit is a financial result, which depends on the two main components, inputs in terms of different costs and output in form of revenues, its evasion is also indirectly connected with overstatement of costs, except payroll, and understatement of revenues. In the following, overstatement of costs and concealment of output will be analyzed aiming mainly at evasion of value-added tax.

Wang and Conant (1988) have considered underreporting of profits through an overstatement of production costs adopting the standard approach of analyzing decision making under uncertainty of the monopolistic

[10] Although they have some deterrent effect, the magnitude of these effects is still unclear (see, Andreoni, J., Erard, B., and Feinstein, J., 1998, p.841-843).

[11] Franzoni, L., 1999, p.62.

firm. Employing a von Neuman-Morgenstern utility function which has profit as its argument (in the good state of the world, tax evasion is not detected; in the bad state the evading firm is caught) they formulate the standard expected utility maximization problem and find the optimal level of output and cost overstatement parameter.

The equilibrium level of output is provided by two conditions: on one hand, it will be larger than output which maximizes profit in the absence of tax; on the other, probability of detection of cost overstatement with further imposition of penalties by the tax authorities offsets this increase of production. By choosing the optimal costs' overstatement parameter, the uncertain monopolist provides the output decision where marginal revenue equals marginal cost, thus not affected by either profit tax or penalty rate. The evasion decision is thus separated from output decision.

Cremer and Gahvari (1993) have analyzed tax evasion in the form of underreporting of sales by competitive firms, which declare only a fraction of their output. The employed structure includes constant marginal cost, consumer price, output level, a specific tax levied on it and tax-enforcement parameters (probability of evasion and the penalty rate on evaded tax). The concealment incurs costs for each unit of output which is represented by the convex function of the proportion of sales concealed. The first and second derivatives of this function are positive. The firm thus maximizes expected profit to determine the optimal level of the output fraction to be declared for the given amount of whole output. The necessary condition for the declared output level equalizes the losses from evading (marginal concealment costs) and gains in terms of the tax on output reduced by the penalty in case of detection.

Further Cremer and Gahvari have defined an expected tax rate, which will be lower in the case of tax evasion activity. It contains a tax levied on the fraction of declared output and an applied penalty if evasion is detected. The firm will always conceal some output if the expected tax rate will be less than the nominal tax rate. The competitive market condition implies equalization of the market price and expected marginal cost, which is comprised of a given constant marginal cost, a cost of concealing and an expected tax rate evaluated at the optimal level of declared output.

The effect of an increase of the tax rate has a negative impact on the level of declared output, consequently, evasion rises, and an ambiguous impact on the expected tax rate. It directly rises since the tax rate increases, but indirectly falls since evasion rises. The impact on the consumer price is definitely positive, but the increase is by less than the amount of tax since some of the increase is absorbed in increased evasion[12]. The increase of the probability of detection leads to positive effects on the level of declared sales, expected tax rate and consumer price. The last impact is seen to have a negative influence on social welfare.

The interesting additional results were derived by Virmani (1989). He investigated the links between evasion and production efficiency, between evasion and firm size and tax thresholds studying firms with U-shaped average costs. Uncertainty is modelled in the expected tax rate, which enters the firm profit function due to maximization. Taking into account the zero-profit condition for competitive firms the equilibrium price is defined. For any given level of evasion the result of profit maximization implies the expansion of the marginal cost of production till it equals consumer price minus tax revenue minus average resource cost of evasion. Since the probability of detection, according to Virmani, increases with the firm's output, a firm can reduce this probability (and marginal effective tax rate) by reducing its output. In equilibrium with evasion a firm does it by producing below than minimum efficient scale associated with minimum average costs leading to production inefficiency.

Virmani defines further a tax rate below which evasion is ruled out (a perfect honesty threshold) and a tax rate above which honesty is ruled out (a complete evasion threshold) in the convex evasion cost case as well as a small scale industry where the minimum optimal scale of production is less than the critical output level at which expected penalty factor equals one. For small firms, the gradual increase of a tax rate from zero will result in transition from complete honesty to complete evasion as the tax rate pass the second threshold. If the linear evasion costs are introduced, only the single tax threshold instead of two appears producing a transition from complete declaration to complete evasion. The increase of the tax rate increases benefits from evasion. If there are no direct costs of evasion, small firms whatever the tax rate is will evade completely which is assumed to be productively inefficient[13].

Marrelli (1984) considered the case of monopoly employing the same structure as Cremer and Gahvari with competitive firms defining a price as chosen by a profit maximizing monopolist. On the one hand, the evasion decision of a monopolist is independent of price setting. On the other hand, the price is determined by the expected cost level, inclusive of tax thus influencing the evasion decision. In the monopoly case the result of tax overshifting occurs. Tax evasion reinforces the rise in price for more than the

[12]Myles, G., 1995, p.407.

[13]See Virmani, A., 1989, p.232.

increase in tax with the increase in tax-enforcement parameters. Marrelli and Martina (1988) derived that in case of oligopolistic firms the evasion decision is independent of the production decisions, on the one hand. On the other hand, the level of production is determined by such factors as the degree of collusion, relative market share of the firms which can influence the evasion decision. Marrelli and Martina proved that increasing collusion leads to a greater evasion.

3.2.3 Profit tax - corporate income tax evasion

Recent developments in the analysis of tax evasion provide additional insights which are specific for tax evasion decisions in corporations. The complication is introduced through separation of ownership and control in the corporate sector resulting in the incompleteness of contract between the owner of the firm and the employed manager, and informational asymmetries when the tax manager is usually more aware of tax evasion (avoidance) opportunities.

The first problem was mainly analyzed by Chen and Chu (2005) while the second one was introduced by Crocker and Slemrod (2005). Both employ approaches to solving mechanism design problems. In the framework provided by Chen and Chu the evasion decision is taken by the owner of the firm, which hires a manager to participate. The contract which should compensate the agent for her efforts and risks is difficult to enforce since the action is illegal. Due to the incompleteness of this contract the manager's incentives can be distorted. So if the owner decides to evade taxes the compensation scheme of the manager is to be changed. So the expected gain from evasion for the firm is not the same as in the Allingham - Sandmo analysis due to the internal control inefficiencies.

The optimization problem of the firm in case of tax evasion consists of two stages: in the first stage the contract is offered to the manager (the only enforceable contact is the contract, which is based on the reported, not actual profits), in the second stage after realizing profits the firm decides how much to declare. Employing the backward induction the authors consider two cases: the manager is not responsible for evasion, and the manager is responsible for tax evasion. In the first case the manager does not need to be compensated for risk, but should be only provided with incentives since she is paid less under the reported income than under real income. Nevertheless there is no loss in internal control due to tax evasion; these two decision-making problems are separable.

But if the manager is liable for tax evasion, there will be efficiency loss in internal control. Actually the agent should be provided with the risk premium contingent on the realized profits which makes her indifferent between participating in evasion and receiving the wage dependable on actual income for sure.

Two types of contract are considered: the original wage contract dependable on reported income with the risk premium and the service contact. The first scheme does not work, because if the premium is paid through the wage contract, the manager has no more incentives to report a lower level of profits. Solving the maximization problem with the incentive compatibility and rationality constraints reveals that efficiency loss in internal control does not occur only if the provision of effort in the first stage is independent of the tax evasion decision in the second stage (the separation of evasion decision and the control of the manager). This is not the case when the manager exhibits increasing or decreasing risk-aversion. Consequently, such factors as good relations or mutual trust can decrease the costs associated with tax evasion, which can also explain the fact why tax evasion is so widespread in small and family firms.

Crocker and Slemrod analyze corporate tax evasion by exploring the effect of penalties on the owner and the tax manager. They assume that the tax manager possesses private information about evasion (avoidance) opportunities of the company, and her incentives to engage in them depend on the compensation scheme. The evidence shows that effective tax rates are one of the most frequently used formal performance measurement[14]. Consequently, the owner can induce the manager to participate in desired evasion by offering him a compensation scheme which equals the saved taxes (permissible and not permissible deductions from the taxable income) minus the costs of evasion incurred by the manager. But in such a case the owner gets no gains from evasion, and the optimal contract in this setting is second-best. In order to extract additional gains from tax evasion the owner must offer the optimal incentive-compatible contract to the manager, but the evasion level will not be efficient in this case. The maximization of corporate profits defined over the range of permissible deductions known to the owner subject to the incentive compatibility and participation constraints of the manager sets up the Hamiltonian function. It captures the total contribution to profits from the choice of legal and illegal reductions of taxable income. The choice of these reductions affects the manager's payoff. The value of change of the manager's payoff is captured by the Lagrangian term, where the Lagrangian multiplier represents the shadow price of the constraint imposed by informational asymmetry, when the manager possesses private information about the level of deductions from taxable income. In this case this level will be lower in comparison with the full information situation. The optimal

[14] See Douglas, R., Ellingsworth, P. and McAndrews, J., 1996.

incentive contract as a function of observed reductions in taxable income is derived and the impact of penalties levied on the owner and the manager by the tax authority is analyzed. The main result is that the penalties levied on the manager will be more effective in reducing the level of tax evasion that suggests using only the agent penalty. This result is due to the second-best compensation contract through which the effect of penalties on shareholders is transmitted to the manager[15].

The analysis of corporate tax evasion focuses on the impact of separation of ownership and control in the corporate sector, which makes the problem more specific. The information constraints cause distortions in the optimal level of tax evasion, setting it at the second-best level.

The theoretical conclusions[16] about specific firm's tax evasion activities explain some features and offer implications for Russia:

1. The expected tax rate serves as an expected rate of return to tax evasion, and the nature and determinants of the concealment cost function is important to explain the firm's non-compliance and capture economic incentives for evasion decision. Low level of concealment costs is associated with higher evasion level.

2. The increase of the probability of detection is proved to be the most effective policy instrument in reducing tax evasion of sales taxes, but its further enforcement may lead to production inefficiencies (for example, under production).

3. The model explains complete evasion of small firms. Normally facing only small direct costs of evasion in Russia, many small and some medium-sized enterprises operate underground.

4. For monopolies, the incurred costs, which include the perceived level of taxation, influence tax evasion decision. So they are more prone to sophisticated evading and avoidance mechanisms. Additionally, for monopolists the output and tax evasion decisions are separable.

5. Increasing collusion among oligopolistic firms leads to greater evasion.

6. In the framework of corporate income tax evasion the problem is captured by the relationship between owners and managers of the firms. Since in Russia managers became owners of companies after privatization the distortions in optimal evasion level caused by information constrains are normally not observed. This fact can also explain higher level of tax evasion in Russian corporations.

[15]Crocker, K., Slemrod, J., 2005, p.1605.

[16]There is practically no empirical analysis of firms' tax evasion (for additional comments see Cowell, F., 2002, p.15-16).

7. Good relations and mutual trust considerably reduce direct costs associated with tax evasion and they are of great importance in Russia.

3.3 Extensions of the basic models: interactions in evasion

3.3.1 Behavioral aspects of tax compliance (interactions between taxpayers)

The models of tax evasion which we considered before do not account for interactions in evading activity. They simply look at the decision-making of an individual (an enterprise) who weights his expected costs and benefits associated with tax evasion and determines whether to evade or not and if yes how much. However, this approach does not allow for other behavioral and institutional aspects which can affect the level of tax evasion in the economy. We consider here the following factors influencing evasion: the role of social norms, combined evasion of income and sales taxes, enforcement mechanism and bribery of tax authorities.

Since some theoretical results could not explain the empirical evidence later studies have tried to introduce terms into the utility function that could also explain the evasion level from the social point of view[17]. Cowell introduced into the utility function of a taxpayer the aggregate level of evasion in the economy, so that the objective function of an evader depends not only on his own evasion level, but on the size of the black economy. It really makes sense on behavioral grounds and it can also substantially reduce the costs of evasion, so the utility level of an evader can rise as the underground economy rises. Considering the corner solutions - complete honesty or complete evasion of a taxpayer depending on the evasion level of the economy with homogeneous population - the equilibria of the economy will be attained either in economy-wide honesty or in complete dishonesty, where the stability of the equilibria is insured by social convention[18]. The intermediate equilibrium where benefits of evasion and honesty are in balance is unstable: exogenous shocks can shift it to corner solutions.

The recent research of Panades (2004) models the utility of a taxpayer, which depends not only on his or her own consumption, but also on the averaged declared income in the economy assuming that the taxpayer derives

[17]Although Sandmo proposed to write the taxpayer's subjective probability of detection as a function both of his own evasion and of his perceived amount of evasion by others (Sandmo, A., 2004, p. 21).

[18]Cowell, F., 1990, p.113.

disutility from declaring more income than the average taxpayer. The weight assigned to this disutility is associated with negative externality, which brings an additional effect. As a result several equilibria arise in the model: for example, the large level of average reported income supposes the small marginal disutility of declaring more income (this utility function depends on the relative tax contribution of the taxpayer (taxpayer's declared income/average declared income in the economy)). For the taxpayer it would be thus optimal to declare a larger amount of income. The comparative static effect of a tax rate's increase depends on the equilibrium: for the "low declaration" equilibrium when the penalties are imposed on the amount of evaded taxes the tax rate's increase leads to more income concealment (opposite to Yitzhaki's result). It is explained that the opposite less income concealment would be heavily penalized if average income reports in the economy are very low. The taxpayer would thus prefer evading more.

Gordon (1989) introduced into the utility function individual psychic costs of evasion resulting in loss of utility due to evasion, which will be more the more taxpayer's evading behavior deviates from that in society. These psychic costs are assumed to be the increasing function of the proportion of non-evading taxpayers. So there are taxpayers who will evade and who do not. The increase of the tax rate can increase the extent of evasion of those who evade and can raise the maximized expected utility of those who do not evade, so that they begin to evade[19].

Bordignon (1993) introduced the fairness constraint of an individual which depends on his tax payment, provided public goods and tax evasion of others. This assessment provides an upper bound of the level of evasion. Then the maximized expected utility of an individual is calculated and the compared smaller amount is evaded. The comparative static effect of a tax rate's increase on the level of evasion is also positive[20].

Myles and Naylor (1996) made a further step in employing the social concept into the standard tax evasion problem. They introduced a social custom utility, which is gained when the person prefers not to evade, and lost when he evades. Consequently, his utility in case of non-evasion is a function of disposable income plus the utility of conforming to the group of taxpayers, which depends on the proportion of those, who do not evade, and the utility obtained following social custom. The latter two (utility of conforming and social custom utility) are also defined as a general function describing the return from the social custom, which are both lost when the tax evasion is chosen. For a given level of reported income the condition for

[19]Gordon, J., 1989, p.804.

[20]Bordignon, M., 1993, p.359.

evasion/non-evasion is specified: the taxpayer evades if the utility derived from evasion is more than this from the honest behavior and does not evade if it is less or equal the utility with no-evasion. Considering an optimal evasion level for the taxpayer for whom the condition holds with equality, the situation of "little" evasion is ruled out. Provided at least one of the "social" functions is positive, the small level of evasion in the interval is allowed so that utility from non-evasion will be greater than the utility from evasion of the small level. Consequently, the optimal level will be greater, so that in the framework with social custom the situation is characterized by the jump to the optimal evasion level once the decision to evade is made.

The result proves that even with a positive expected financial gain from evasion, there will be those, who do not evade. With this in mind the critical proportion of evading taxpayers is determined. If this point is less than the amount of evaders in the economy, the taxpayer with his evaluations of the utility of conforming and of social custom will evade, if more, than he will pay all taxes. The corner solutions show that if all people in the economy are evaders, but the taxpayer's utility from non-evasion is more or equal to the utility if he evades, then he will always pay a full amount of taxes. If, on the contrary, all agents are honest (the critical proportion of evading taxpayers is zero), but the expected utility of the individual taxpayer is more when he evades, he will always evade taxes. Defining the function of the critical proportion of evaders depends on evaluation of the conforming and social custom utility of the taxpayer who chooses to evade, and deriving the utility of social custom as the function of monotonic transformation of the former, those who evade will have this social custom utility less than the function which will characterize the equilibrium level of evasion.

Summing all over potential evades with different social evaluations, the social equilibrium and its possible forms are defined: non evasion, full evasion, the situation when simultaneously both cases hold, which is actually unlikely and the situation when both cases do not hold, which is more observable in reality. The instability of the no-evasion equilibrium is stated: it can disappear by small changes in tax rates or in income level, which can lead to the interior equilibrium characterized by the certain extent of evasion. Under certain assumptions these changes can have a positive, as well as a negative effect, on the number of evading taxpayers and the evasion level. The heterogeneity of income does not change the results of the model.

A nice approach to modelling the social convention was suggested by Cullis and Lewis (1997). Social norms are modelled as public goods, in which consumption, production and investment choice are captured. The price of conformity to social norms is captured by the cost of due tax payments of a taxpayer in view of general tax compliance in society and by the cost of not being a free-rider. For example, the price of conformity is higher if in case of the low tax compliance in society the taxpayer is faced with a higher tax rate and suffers more costs, as not being a free rider in a society where the utility of honesty is very low. Taxpayers demand the amount of conformity dependent on the price observed, which they can influence through their investment choice. The level of societal investment in conformity is converted by the production process to the price of conformity. For example, reduction in investment can be expressed by resistance to pay taxes, in failure to register with tax organs. Production depends in its turn on the level of past investments in conformity, on the tax collection process and its efficiency (for example, corruption in tax organs reduces this efficiency).

Individual and social equilibria differ in the price of conformity and quantity demanded. In a social equilibrium, consumption externalities are internalized. This "consumption" externality is expressed through the taxpayer's perception that he or she contributes to tax compliance, but sees that others still do not fulfill their tax obligations. Different levels of conformity can be observed even if the public goods problem in the investment process is solved. This softer approach focuses on the importance of behavioral aspects expressed in attitudes, values, fiscal consciousness, social norms, conformity and voluntary nature of tax compliance. Based on the conformity to social conventions, the structure explains a whole set of reasons why tax compliance can fail in society leading to the so called "bad" equilibrium characterized by epidemics of tax evasion. Malfunctioning of the investment process is typically "free riding" of those who do not comply with the tax system. Since the government is seen as the main solver of public goods' problem, it should create and support an institutional framework which would foster tax compliance: the performance of the state in the provision of public goods, protection of property rights, creation of the "rule of law", redistributional aspects. Then the system must be able to utilize the undertaken investments through the process, which produces compliance norms: the corresponding tax structure, efficiency of tax authorities. And at last, if the consumption externality is not internalized in the lower "social" price of conformity, lower level of demanded social norms is observed and non-compliance is reinforced. So there are many interior equilibria to be considered, and the economy like this of Russia ends up in a "bad" equilibrium.

There are also attempts to develop a psychological theory of tax evasion. In his model Vihanto (2000) assumes that taxpayers are unable to optimize their behavior due to their limited knowledge or cognitive skills. He assumes, for example, that the decision of a taxpayer to evade is based on the good results produced in the past. It can be his experience or the experience of his friends who have cheated successfully. Instead of optimizing under uncertainty, the taxpayer resorts to backward-looking. The game theoretic approach also confirms that those who just begin to play a game usually experiment through losses. They learn gradually, also by imitating the actions of more experienced players. Vihanto argues that society can follow honest behavior and does not evade if they consent on the social contract where tax rules find unanimous approval of the people[21].

Introducing social norms enriches the basic analysis and has some explanations of the Russian situation:

1. The taxpayer's subjective probability of detection or his utility can change if they are assumed to be functions of the perceived evasion by others in the economy. The optimal level of evasion thus changes, and the process is characterized by the multiple equilibria.

2. The Russian case represents the so called "bad" equilibrium marked by the epidemics of evasion, which persists. The stability of this "bad" equilibrium, guaranteed by the social convention, predicts the complexities while combating tax evasion.

3. The approach explains the main failure of the government to guarantee tax compliance in the society from the beginning of the transition period. It fails to meet the needs of society to provide public goods. Privatization process produced the reluctance of firms to "invest" in social norms.

4. It also helps to understand other interactions in the tax evading activity of firms: collusion of the evaders with each other and with tax authorities. Corruption and extortion aggravate the latter aspect.

3.3.2 Joint tax evasion (interactions in transactions)

Based on joint cheating, Fedeli and Forte (1999) explored the interactions in evasion between taxpayers, when firms negotiate about transactions. They consider a chain consisting of two firms, a shop and a purchaser, who bargain about the understating of their receipts and costs thus evading value-added and income tax simultaneously. Their income tax base is defined as a difference between receipts and costs, and the VAT transferred to the state as a difference between VAT obtained on receipts and VAT paid on costs (for simplicity, labor costs and investments are not taken into account). The gain from evasion is only possible if the second player (the second firm) in the chain agrees to accept invoices with lower sums. By understating his costs, this player must be sure he can persuade the next player (the shop) to accept the understated receipts. Otherwise the tax bases for the second player would

[21]See Vihanto, M., 2000, p.29-30.

be more than without evasion; additionally it also means the probability of being caught and penalized that makes evasion even more unprofitable.

Using the Nash bargaining, the functions in the form of product of net gains from the illegal trade for the two agents are defined: between the firm 1 and 2, the firm 2 and the shop, and the shop and the consumer. Considering payoffs of all agents in the chain, the equilibrium share of evasion is determined by using backward induction. It is assumed that the consumer is willing to accept understated receipts, although he does not receive further gains from the black transaction, since he is a final payer in the chain and can't claim VAT refund.

Returning to the model's assumption that the consumer accepts VAT evasion, the Nash bargaining solution between the shop and the consumer is defined; the equilibrium share of evasion is thus the maximized product of the net gains from the black trade obtained at the last stage of the chain. After an equilibrium has been determined at the last stage , we can substitute the amount of evaded receipts of the shop into the function of the bargain between the firm 2 and the shop to obtain the equilibrium bargaining share of receipts' evasion for the firm 2. Analogously, the equilibrium amount of evasion between firm 1 and 2 is defined. Comparing these three equilibria, the highest level of evasion is observed at the last stage. This result leads to the immediate policy implication that the chain could be stopped if the strategy would be to deter the evasion at this last stage.

Actually it would be very easy at the first sight, since the consumer is ready to accept understated receipts from the shop if the VAT rate is equal or greater than the product of the probability of being inspected by the tax authority and penalty rates for VAT evasion - all the parameters are under control of the tax organs and not connected with the amounts of receipts and costs evaded. Consequently, since the penalties should be fair, the most effective policy to combat VAT evasion is to increase the number of inspections by controlling the transactions which the consumer makes.

Fedeli and Forte claim that this sort of police-state is not a good policy consequence. Moreover, in reality it is more often the case that the consumers do not actually gain from black trade. Prevalently, they simply do not claim receipts on their purchases. If sellers see this opportunity and cash transactions are widespread, venders do not negotiate with consumers at all. The consumers' rationality constraint (if they perceive that the VAT rate is more than the probability of being caught and penalized) does not play any role. Nevertheless, the result of the model that the most effective instrument for reducing VAT (also income tax) evasion is increasing the probability of detection seems to be rather predictable, since VAT is considered to be the most easily administered tax.

The authors derive a condition when it is made unprofitable for the shop to bargain with the firm 2 in which case the chain of evasion is also stopped. They propose to differentiate inspections by increasing the probability of detection and penalty rates for VAT compared to income tax[22]. All these measures require the availability of skilled tax inspectors. Moreover, through more control, the probability of another kind of interaction between tax evaders and tax authorities increases, which may potentially lead to corruption.

The implications of the model are the following:

1. The possibility of collusion reinforces the hypothesis of epidemics of evasion. In this concern such factors as relational capital and mutual trust which characterize the Russian system contribute to the higher evasion level in the economy.

2. Efficient control and enforcement is proved to be a good policy instrument to deter joint evasion, but a police state seems not to be a good solution. Moreover, it can provoke bad government practices such as corruption and extortion.

3.3.3 Evasion and enforcement (interactions between taxpayers and tax authorities)

We have already mentioned in the analysis of the basic Allingham-Sandmo framework that the model incorporates only two instruments of enforcement such as penalty and audit rate. Moreover, the probability of audit is constant, which in principle does not need to be the same for all taxpayers. The subsequent theory thus assumes the probability of audit to be the function of reported income. In this framework two types of models are to be distinguished: in the first case the tax authority commits to its previously announced audit policy, in the second case they decide which taxpayers to audit after all returns have been filed.

Reinganum and Wilde (1985) analyzed the audit policy which maximizes tax revenues by making it conditional on the level of reported liability. They derive a cut-off rule which sets a threshold above which income reports are not audited and below which they are audited with some probability. The purpose of setting this threshold is to deter those who earn more from reporting the threshold level of income also by setting the probability of this audit high enough that these individuals will be indifferent to reporting the threshold level of income or their next best alternative income (which may

[22]Fedeli, S., Forte, F., 1999, p.409.

be their true income)[23]. The authors showed that this rule dominates the random audit rule implied by the model of Allingham and Sandmo. The result shows that audits should serve primarily as a deterrent from tax evasion, and not as an instrument of punishment.

In their subsequent research Reinganum and Wilde (1986) presented a model as a game of incomplete information, when a taxpayer first reports the income, and at the next stage tax authorities act optimally on the basis of this information. They have found that, in equilibrium, greater efforts should be put to verify the taxpayers with lower incomes, so that optimal audit rule should decline with reported income[24].

Andreoni, Erard and Feinstein (1998) provided a critical analysis of these kinds of models focusing on the facts that they poorly describe real-world tax systems and are not supported empirically[25]. It is also evident that apart from penalties and audit probabilities, institutional features of real enforcement also matter. In this context we consider corruption which influences enforcement and thus the level of tax evasion.

3.3.4 Corruption and tax evasion

Interactions between taxpayers and tax authorities introduce a special part of the problem of tax evasion where strategic behavior plays a dominant role. The chance which the taxpayer takes by evasion is dependent on the tax collector's behavior: whether to undertake an inspection or not; if yes, whether to be bribed or not. The taxpayer's behavior whether to evade taxes or not will take into account the possibility of being investigated. Even if this probability would be equal to one, it would not discourage the taxpayer to dodge due taxes if he knows he can bribe the tax collector.

The so called "rate of return" of tax evasion is not known to firms, it actually lies in government's hands (or its tax authorities). In this sense the uncertainty can be considered as endogenous.

As an example we take the game between a firm and tax authorities, where the taxpayer decides to evade or not to evade, and the tax inspector decides to investigate or not. There is no equilibrium in pure strategies since if a firm does not evade the tax authorities prefer not investigating; if not investigated, the firm will switch to evasion. Assigning the corresponding probabilities, the Nash equilibrium in mixed strategies can be found where the probability of evasion increases with the costs of investigation[26]. If the

[23] Andreoni, J. et.al., 1998, p.828.

[24] Reinganum, J., Wilde, L., 1986, p.755.

[25] For further details on critical discussion see Andreoni, J. et.al., 1998, p.831-834.

[26] See Cowell, F., 1990, p.120.

taxpayer anticipates high costs of investigation his probability to evade is expected to increase.

The fact that government (or its tax authorities) is corrupt may also influence the probability of tax evasion; moreover, conventional sanctions against tax evaders may not have the desired effect in the long run - if the penalty for evasion is increased, then all that may happen is that the equilibrium price of bribery may rise while everyone carries on as before[27].

Corruption is widely researched by many economists[28], as well as the impact it exerts on the shadow economy. Yet there are definitely less studies which model tax evasion and corruption simultaneously.

The one of such approaches was developed by Bowels (2000). He assumes risk neutrality and defines the expected cost of taking a bribe as a product of the probability of detection by anti-corruption division and punishment costs. By linking the bribe and its costs to tax inspectors he defined the proportion of corrupt tax officials. For the taxpayer the maximum amount of bribe will equal the penalties on undeclared income. Assuming that they reach a bargain, the bribe will be on the midway between the maximum amount of bribe the taxpayer will be ready to offer and the expected costs of taking it for the tax inspector. Then the evasion decision of the taxpayer is determined: for him the payoff in case of honest declaration should be more than the expected terms which take into account the following possibilities: investigation by the corrupt tax collector, who is caught at the next stage; investigation by the corrupt inspector, who is not caught by taking the bribe; investigation by the honest official and no investigation at all. The psychic costs when evading are derived from the taxpayer's expected payoffs. These costs define the critical point below which evasion takes place. The condition depends on a set of exogenous parameters, such as tax rate, penalties, probability of detection, income and the probability of corruption being checked, and endogenous ones such as the level of bribe and the proportion of corrupt officials defined above. The corresponding comparative static effects are the following: the tax rate's increase induces more evasion, the probability of investigation and the penalty rate's increase reduces tax evasion, whereas an increase in the probability of being caught by taking a bribe causes ambiguity on the evasion level. This surprising effect is explained by the fact that the increase of the expected costs of taking a bribe results in increase of the level of bribes, which in turn can encourage more tax inspectors to corruptive activity. It is not also always clear why the increase in penalty rate reduces

[27] Cowell, F., 1990, p.192.

[28] See, for example, Schleifer, A. and Vishny, R. (1993), Kaufmann, D. (2001), Tanzi, V. (2000), Fjeldstad, O.-H. and Tungodden, B. (2003).

evasion. The bribe gets expensive, but it will be easier to find the corrupt inspector, with whom the taxpayer can bargain more tax evasion. The whole income can be evaded as one can observe in reality. What actually determines the results of this model are the psychic costs of evasion, which are themselves dependable on the set of certain parameters.

The model of Hindriks, Keen and Muthoo (1999) combines evasion and corruption activities of taxpayers and inspectors whereby the optimal tax policy design is incorporated and the traditional equity-efficiency trade-off is considered. In their model they assume the possibility of extortion (the practice often observed in reality, when the bribe is taken even if the taxpayer does not evade), the payment of commission to tax inspectors for higher income reports and non-linear tax schedules.

The three-stage game is derived thus: the announcement of the tax scheme by the government, income reporting and appeal, and at the last stage, the detection by the anti-corruption body is allowed. In the second stage when the taxpayer is investigated, evasion becomes common knowledge between the tax collector and the taxpayer. They bargain according to the game form consisting of the agreed payment to the state and the level of bribe payment (it is a side-contract since the government can not control and choose the game form). In case of disagreement the tax collector chooses the level of reported income himself which the taxpayer can appeal incurring additional fixed costs. The agreement is Pareto efficient if the surplus of the expected payoffs of both players is maximized.

The authors show that in this case the players play better than in the disagreement game. The employed game form distinguishes evasion and corruption: the former supposes the understatement of income reported to the state, the latter - the bribe different from zero. With the commission paid to tax inspectors on higher income reports, they are needed to be bribed in order to tolerate tax evasion since they lose their commission and can potentially be penalized. The proposition thus states that tax evasion implies corruption. But corruption does not imply tax evasion, because the model does not exclude the overstatement of the income in equilibrium (the case of extortion). Furthermore, such cases occur if the tax inspectors are paid on commission and if the appeal process is imperfect[29].

Consequently, under the commission scheme those who earn high income normally evade, while the low income group is vulnerable to extortions. Moreover, the authors define the equilibrium bribe as a function of income, which is increasing for the low income group, constant for the middle class and decreasing for the high income group, concluding that the middle

[29]The second reason can partly explain the cases of extortions in Russia.

class pays the highest level of bribes. They point out at the regressive effect which evasion and corruption exacerbate making progressive taxation less equitable.

The rest of the paper is concerned with the consideration of policy options and tax schemes in order to combat evasion and corruption. The most acute problem about the level of penalties and its impact on the level of bribe is analyzed firstly: it was shown that if the tax inspector extorts, the increase in penalties can decrease the level of corruption, but if the players collude about evasion, the corresponding effect is ambiguous: here the observed effect of demanding more for collusion (since the cost of taking a bribe has increased) is offset by an increase in the agreed level of taxation, which reduces the bribe. The increase in commission payment on higher income reports reduces the tax evasion, but this increase in tax revenues is offset by the increased costs of the commission payments.

Taking into consideration the previous results, the optimal tax scheme which corresponds to the four government objectives - revenue maximization, combat of evasion and corruption, and distributional aspects - is analyzed. For the implementation of the first objective, the probability of corruption being detected is of primary importance; this probability is described as "a degree of intrinsic honesty in the system". The commissions to inspectors presenting the higher income reports can reduce the level of evasion, but considering corruption issues these commissions can induce extortion, which can be precluded by simply paying no commissions at all, or at least on low income reports. Thus, the optimal tax scheme proposed should rule out the progressivity of income taxation in the lower part of income distribution. Furthermore, over reporting could be also ruled out by setting the costs of appeals very low for the taxpayer or by setting the expected punishment very high (the costs of appeal and the probability of checking corruption are exogenously given in the model).

Examining the distributional aspects of the tax system, the proportional tax schedule and progressive schedule above some critical point of income are compared. It is pointed out that although the honest implementation of the progressive scheme by tax inspectors paid on commission for high income reports reduces tax evasion, the tax burden of such a scheme is definitely higher. The government thus must trade off the equitable (progressive) tax system against less efficient (with higher tax burden) tax scheme.

The conclusions to be made are the following:

1. Cultural factors such as social networks, relationships, strong links between state and non-state sector are of great importance for analyzing tax evasion in Russia. Consequently, interactions between taxpayers, tax

collectors and the state, especially when allowing for corruption or extortion, play a considerable role in modifying the level of tax evasion in the economy[30].

2. If corruption is possible, firms' tax evasion may be facilitated.

3. Since comparative static analysis provides no clear-cut answer to how to reduce tax evasion and corruption, such parameters as the probability of corruption being detected, the costs of appeal (as well as the rule of law), the psychic costs of evasion or weight which is assigned to corruptive activities in the society, which are usually exogenously given in the models, play a key role in policy analysis of combating tax evasion and corruption.

4. Modelling different remuneration schemes for tax inspectors (from tax-farming till pure wage scheme) also do not give an answer as to which of them is better suited for reducing corruption in tax administration and the evasion level. When all tax inspectors are corruptible it is proved to be optimal to pay them shares of their tax collections (pure tax-farming)[31]. But if extortion is allowed (the costs of appeal are very high as it is observed in Russia), this result does not hold anymore.

5. The increase in penalties is proved to produce an ambiguous effect if the players can collude, because it can cause an increase in bribe payment.

3.4 Optimal taxation issues in the presence of tax evasion and tax policy design

The literature on optimal taxation has found its extensions by incorporating the tax evasion problem into the standard framework of optimal income taxation and optimal commodity taxation. As far as the taxation of business income is concerned, we will consider it separately in the last section of this chapter under the neutral business tax or the tax on inframarginal profits (economic rents), where the aspects of tax evasion are taken into account.

Cremer and Gahvari (1995) presented the modified model of Mirrlees (1971), in which tax evasion is incorporated. In the standard framework they assume that the true income of two types of individuals (low wage and high wage) can be only observed through costly audits and that the labor supply is endogenized. Two opportunities for evasion arise: persons can pretend they are of another type, which can not be detected by audit, or they misreport their income which can be discovered through costly auditing. It is quite evident, that compared with the traditional setting, policy on tax evasion can never be optimal since the amount of required revenues is increased by

[30] According to Tanzi, V. (1998) social capital provides fertile ground for corruption.

[31] Wane, W., 2000, p.30.

the costs of observation due to audits. Consequently, optimal policies should aim to reduce these costs by choosing optimal audit probabilities but not reducing social welfare (the objective function of the government) at the same time .

The main results are as follows:

- no audits for high income persons. This result is obtained due to the risk aversion of individuals, whose expected utility would increase were the taxes more certain. The decrease of audit costs is also provided.

- the probability of audit less than one for low income persons. If it were one, there would be no incentives for taxpayers to cheat. The result also improves welfare since the audit costs are lowered. The aim of the government is to prevent the rich imitating low income individuals, but not to audit the poor, because from the beginning the government does not know who is who.

- "no distortion at the top" also applies in this framework;

- honest reporting should be rewarded. The negative effect of costly differentiation is outweighed by the positive effect of reporting more honestly. If it is not possible due to the principle of horizontal equity, the results of the model still hold.

- it is also possible not to distort the behavior of low income persons under some constraints. So despite extension of evasion, qualitative characteristics of the standard income tax schedule remain valid, which may be seen as an indirect argument against lower marginal tax rates in the presence of evasion[32].

Myles (1995) provides an interesting result of deriving the Ramsey rule in case of tax evasion. The only difference is that the consumer price is defined as a sum of a constant marginal cost, the tax evasion cost and the expected tax payment dependent on a nominal tax rate of the good. Additionally auditing costs dependent on probabilities of detection are defined. The sum of compensated demand changes contains now an additional term which measures the relative increase of the expected tax rate to price when a nominal tax rate of the good is raised. In the absence of tax evasion this term equals one showing that price rises by the amount of increased tax. With evasion the stronger increase of the expected tax rate relative to the price due to the raised tax rate provides more reduction in compensated demand and because of the greater increase of the effective tax rate - less incentives for tax evasion. This implies heavier taxation of goods with a greater relative change in compensated demands, and more broadly - differentiated commodity taxation. But as it can be observed in Russia, for example, in case of tax duties

[32]Pirttilae, J., 1999, p.16.

which are quite differentiated, this policy practice leads to false declaration of goods to which lower rates are applied if tax and customs officials are corrupt.

Newbery (1997) addresses the problem of tax design in transition economies in the conditions of constant tax reforms and tax evasion. The structure he employs looks the following: he abstracts from profit tax and converts commodity taxes into their income tax equivalent (since the optimal indirect tax should fall on final consumption and not distort production decisions). Additionally, the tax system is represented by a uniform grant (transfer) and the fixed revenue requirement. As a starting point Newbery assumes that the uniform commodity taxes and lump-sum grant are optimal (following the results of Deaton, Atkinson and Stiglitz)[33]. The optimal tax problem is stated in the usual way: the optimization of social welfare function summed over individual indirect utility functions under the constraint that a certain amount of revenues should be collected. In the constraint it is assumed that only a part of goods is covered by indirect (value-added) tax due to evasion. Calculating the model with the parameters shows that reduced VAT coverage increases the marginal costs of raising revenues. The effect is expressed in a reduction of the level of the redistributive expenditure. Additionally to VAT evasion, income tax evasion is introduced: it is assumed that only a proportion of taxpayers are paying their income taxes. By specifying the extent of both types of evasion and varying the proportional rate of income tax, the VAT rate is optimized. At the end the pair of tax rates which maximizes social welfare is selected. The main result is that if VAT coverage is complete there is no need for income tax. If it is incomplete, then income tax can complement VAT even if it is evaded. The overall tax coverage can be increased and the collection costs lowered.

Many economists say that income taxes are easy to evade, consequently, the government should rely more on indirect taxes, value-added tax in particular[34]. Before proceeding with the conclusions, one aspect of tax systems deserves attention: its complexity. On the one hand, it is politically rational to facilitate the complex tax system[35]. On the other hand, the empirical study conducted by Thiessen (2003) for the Ukrainian economy showed that tax complexities (together with regulatory burden and soft-budget constraint) are important causes of the shadow economy's growth. These simplicity and clarity considerations, should be also taken into account by designing the optimal tax system and are highly relevant for Russian tax policy implications.

[33] This result holds only if the substantial restrictions are put on preferences. Actually consumers should be identical.

[34] See, for example, Gordon, R. and Nielsen, S., 1997.

[35] See, Hettich and Winer, 1988.

Some conclusions can be derived from optimal taxation issues:

1. In Russia, where most part of individual income taxes are paid on the withholding basis, the results of evasion's implications for optimal income taxation are of limited value. Nevertheless, they point out at the non-optimality of very high probability of audits.

2. In the presence of tax evasion, the standard income tax schedule remains valid. This fact may not favor the application of lower marginal tax rates in the optimal tax analysis.

3. The differentiated commodity taxation implied by the optimal theory is hardly applicable in Russia due to the weak tax administration and the discretion which they apply.

4. Apart from efficiency, simplicity and clarity of tax law should also be taken into account in tax policy design. It may potentially deter the application of arbitrary rules by tax officials.

3.5 Taxation of economic rents

So far optimal income and optimal commodity taxation in the presence of tax evasion were discussed. Corporate income tax is additionally among the most evaded taxes. In the following we will consider tax on inframarginal (pure) profits or economic rents. There is not much literature on taxation of economic rents but nevertheless taxation of rents is shown to have some useful properties, also in the presence of tax evasion.

Bond and Devereux (1995, 2003) analyzed business tax levied on pure profits or economic rents, which is neutral with respect to investment decisions of value-maximizing firms, and which is informationally feasible to implement.

In the simple setting the one-period model could be presented in the following way. To show the neutrality of the tax structure the business concept of net present value is employed, which is actually considered as pure profit (economic rents) on which the business tax is levied. The net present value (NPV) is the difference between the expected income flows earned by the asset (Π) discounted at the rate of return offered by equivalent investment alternatives (i) and required investment (K)[36]. The risk neutrality is assumed.

$$NPV = V - K, \tag{3.1}$$

where $V = \frac{\Pi}{(1+i)}$ or

[36]Brealey, R., Myers, S., 2000, p.17.

$$(1+i)V = \Pi. \tag{3.2}$$

If the income from the asset is taxed at tax rate t and capital income from all other sources at m, there are tax deductions for depreciation D and the opportunity cost of finance's tax allowance F, then the economic value of this asset from (3.2) in the presence of tax is given by

$$(1+(1-m)i)V = (1-t)\Pi + t(D+F).$$

The right-hand side of the equation is the post-tax income from the asset; the left-hand side is the post-tax income from the alternative use of the same funds.

In the setting where $m = 0$ (the interest income is not taxed at all), $D = K$ (the depreciation allowance is given on the sum of required investment) and $F = iK$ (the opportunity cost of finance's deduction is given), the economic value is given as

$$(1+i)V = (1-t)\Pi + t(1+i)K$$

$$V = \frac{(1-t)\Pi}{(1+i)} + tK \tag{3.3}$$

Inserting (3.3) into (3.1) we will get

$$NPV = (1-t)[\frac{\Pi}{(1+i)} - K] \tag{3.4}$$

After simplifying $NPV = (1-t)NPV$.

The neutral business tax exempts the required return on investments and taxes only economic rents[37]. So the returns on investment are not taxed and neutrality is provided. It means that tax rate would not affect the sign of the post-tax NPV, and therefore, tax will not affect investment decision. Value-maximizing investment decisions are not distorted.

In their most recent paper Bond and Devereux (2003) consider two general business tax structures: one on the net present value generated by the firm and the other on the net present value captured by the shareholders, the difference between which is in the deductibility of the interest expenses in case of the shareholder tax. The interest deductibility is a feature of modern tax systems. Bond and Devereux also proved the neutrality of both taxes

[37] See Bond, S., Devereux, M., 1995, p.5.

in the presence of uncertainty and the probability of wind-up (liquidation). They assume the perfect competitive capital markets with symmetric information where the providers of debt finance earn only a normal return on their investment and consequently earn no economic rents. The economic rents are wholly captured by the firm's shareholders.

By summarizing the features of the firm tax it can be inferred that revenues (cash inflows) net of operating costs are taxed at the constant tax rate, whereby the deduction for the costs of the assets is allowed (100 percent depreciation allowance). If this 100 percent depreciation allowance is not carried out in the initial period, in the subsequent periods the firm should be compensated by additional provision of the opportunity cost of finance's allowance equal the value of the costs deductible discounted at the risk-free nominal rate of interest in the period. Consequently, all the information the tax authorities should know in order to implement this tax, is cash inflows from the real activity of the firm (and distinguish them from the cash inflows which serve to finance this real activity) and the nominal rate of interest. Provided these income flows, especially in the case of a natural resource industry which is mainly export-oriented, are very well observable, the problem of tax evasion could be alleviated and potentially resolved.

The features of the shareholder tax look as such: the revenues net of operating costs taxed at the constant tax rate, 100 percent depreciation allowance, the cost of equity finance's allowance, the allowance for interests paid, but the taxation of interest received. Since financial receipts are also taxed, to provide neutrality the lenders' net financial receipts should be also taxed at the same rate (for example, if interest payments are deductible for the firm, they should be taxed by the debt provider). As it is seen, the situation looks more complicated with shareholder tax since in order for this tax to be neutral, more elements in the tax structure are needed and consequently more informational requirements. Additionally, on the credit markets with imperfect competition the implementation of shareholder tax imposes extra problems such as the ability of debt providers with market power to set the interest rate higher than perfectly competitive, or the possibility of collusion between the firm and the lender leading to tax evasion[38]. The mentioned problem is acute for Russia, where companies often have their own banks with the help of which the tax evasion schemes are implemented.

Summing up the features of optimal business tax in the presence of tax evasion we note the following:

1. The tax should fall on pure profit (economic rents) or net present value.

[38]See Bond, S.R., Devereux, M.P., 2003, p.1304-1305.

2. It should be neutral, i.e. should not influence investment decisions.

3. Since evasion of corporate income tax presupposes distortions of many costs and revenues by firms, it is very difficult to keep track of. Consequently, minimum information is needed to calculate the tax.

3.6 Summary

The models which explain tax evasion can be divided into those which directly concern the decision of the taxpayer to evade taxes and the ones which model the particular economic environment in which the incentives to evade taxes are exacerbated.

For Russia the privatization process activated incentives to economic agents which gave rise to massive tax evading activities. It did not actually separate management from owners and state from non-state activities. Consequently, it did not happen that the new owners began to demand the rule-of-law from the state as it was initially expected. Moreover, the winners of privatization are interested in prolonging the "no-rule-of-law" regime in which state authorities on all levels are not restricted to taking arbitrary actions. In such an environment tax compliance is hardly expected. Implicit tax rates were set also very high.

Social welfare theories of tax evasion point that higher tax rates may increase tax evasion, although in some settings (when taxes are withheld by the employer) this effect is indeterminate. The increase of enforcement parameters reduce tax evasion, but increasing the probability of detection may compel a competitive firm to decrease its output (if this probability increases with the firm's output) below efficient scale and provoke some sort of police-state as well. If there are no direct costs of evasion, small firms can completely evade taxes. The decision of monopolies to evade taxes is more influenced by the incurred concealment costs; they also separate output and evasion decisions. The lack of information constraints (no separation of management and owners), good relations and mutual trust inside Russian companies considerably reduce the direct costs associated with tax evasion and facilitate the tax evasion decision.

The models of tax evasion with social norms explain the situation where the country is in "bad" equilibrium characterized by the high evasion level. The stability of this equilibrium is guaranteed by social convention. The system based on so called relational capital makes collusion among involved agents more possible which also facilitates tax evasion.

The corresponding incentive structure governing the conduct of law enforcers affects the actual functioning of all enforcement tools and, consequently, the level of tax evasion. If, for example, corruption is possible at the investigation stage, some part of tax evasion can be facilitated. Such aspects as the probability of corruption's detection, the costs of appeal, psychic costs of evasion gain importance in policy analysis. Standard instruments such as the increase of penalties for tax evasion produce an ambiguous effect if the players can collude.

Optimal income taxation theory in the presence of tax evasion does not result in high audit probabilities and, indirectly, the lower marginal tax rates. The differentiated commodity taxation implied by the modified Ramsey rule is hardly applicable in Russia since it can be misused by the enforcers. Instead simplicity and clarity of the tax law as well as the minimum information requirement for taxes' calculation is encouraged which may potentially deter the application of arbitrary rules by state officials and reduce corruption and extortion among them. Tax on business profits (economic rents) is recommended in this respect.

Chapter 4

Corporate evasion and governments

The in-depth country analysis of tax evasion in Russia highlighted some specific features of this phenomenon, whereas theoretical investigations propose the policy implications for fighting tax evasion in general. In this chapter we try to combine tax evasion diagnostics with theoretical findings to see whether it can offer some results in a particular country-specific environment. As corruption and extortion were identified as one of the main causes of tax evasion in Russia, we consider further the interdependence between these aspects and corporate tax evasion decisions in the theoretical context.

Paragraph 4.1 considers corporate tax evasion when the government is prone to extortion. We distinguish between two types of government: the good one which is interested in detecting and penalizing for tax evasion, and a bad one which extorts monies from firms. In the static model we introduce only the uncertainty about the government type; in the dynamic setting the firm also holds private information about its profitability. Additionally, the case when extortion may be costly for a bad government is considered. Our primary interest will be to explore influence of extortion on corporate tax evasion and analyze effects of tax policy parameters such as tax rates, penalties and audits on tax evasion.

In paragraph 4.2 we consider mechanisms of corporate tax evasion. They consist of cost and profit manipulation. We are interested in analyzing the policy parameters which influence corporate benefits of tax evasion. Decreased taxes on profit and labor as well as increased concealment costs may help to reduce these benefits. But as long as incentives to manipulate profits, labor and other costs are not removed, a firm will still evade taxes. Moreover, as the state "participates" in tax evasion by practicing corruption and extortion in its bodies, the problem of tax evasion is particularly difficult to handle. We propose a tax regime where incentives for a firm to distort its costs and profits can be alleviated. Discretion of tax authorities can be also reduced. This regime is a decision rule set up by the state which defines a tax rate on the basis of share of labor costs as a proportion of total costs.

4.1 Tax evasion and extortionist governments

4.1.1 Introduction and literature

The right of governments to exercise fiscal power through taxation sometimes leads to its abuse by public officials. Tax enforcement provides a very powerful tool for extortion in countries where the government has control over enforcing agencies and courts. Extortion can take the form of overstated tax obligations or arbitrary financial punishment of (non-existent) tax evasion by firms[1]. On one hand, extortion is considered as a special form of corruption, its most serious form. Since corruption is defined by the World Bank as "the abuse of public office for private gain"[2], extortion can be interpreted as corruption. On the other hand, it is standard in the literature[3] to distiguish extortion as a bad government practice in which public officials require money even if a firm does not commit tax evasion.

It is easier for a malicious government to control enforcement agencies and courts if law institutions are week and/or a lack of separation of power exists. Week institutions allow for control through bribery, while the lack of separation of power provides leeway for direct influence. Both corrupt courts and the lack of checks and balances is readily observed in developing and transition economies. These countries quite regularly suffer from problems to create sufficient revenues from taxation. So it is interesting to investigate the influence of potentially extortionist governments on tax revenues and enforcement cost.

---

[1]The Russian YUKOS case is considered by many observers as such government extortion. Mikhail Khodorkovsky, owner of energy giant YUKOS was jailed for 9 years after he was found guilty of tax evasion. The most profitable parts of the firm were auctioned off in order to settle the tax repayments. In the intransparent auction a firm with Kremlin links purchased the assets. US congressman Tom Lantos commented: "It seems that this political trial before a kangaroo court has come to a shameful conclusion." See the BBC's website for further details (http://news.bbc.co.uk/1/hi/business/4595289.stm).

[2]See World Bank 1997, p.8.

[3]See, for example, Hindriks, J., Keen, M., Muthoo, A., Corruption, Extortion, Evasion, 1999.

So far, the not particularly extensive literature on corporate tax evasion has mainly focused on the influence of tax evasion and enforcement on production decisions[4]. Recently, the organizational structure of firms and its influence on tax evasion has been analyzed by Chen and Chu (2002) and by Crocker and Slemrod (2004). The papers most closely related to our analysis are Hindriks, Keen and Muthoo (1999), who propose an optimal tax system in the presence of evasion, corruption and extortion, and Cule and Fulton (2005), who explain the positive correlation between evasion and corruption by the complementary nature of the shadow economy and corruption activity.

We model the tax evasion decision of a firm if it is uncertain about the kind of government it faces. A government may be "good" or "bad", where a good government just wants to collect revenue and to prevent tax evasion, while a bad government engages in extortion. In the static game the firm and the government simultaneously take their action "evade, not evade" and "penalize, not penalize" respectively. We find that the equilibrium belief about the government type depends solely on penalties the good government imposes on tax evaders, and not on extortion parameter of the bad type of government. The higher the probability of bad government, the higher the level of tax evasion. If bribery if possible to escape extortion, tax evasion starts to pay for lower levels of probability of bad government. Consequently, tax evasion incentives are even more exacerbated.

In the dynamic setting a firm decides on its profit declaration for tax purposes, while being uncertain about the objective of the government. The government observes declaration and takes its action. We find that the prior probability of facing an extortionist government increases tax-evasion incentives. Therefore the potential for extortion undermines revenue collection of good governments. Moreover, the prior probability of firms facing a bad government increases the expected equilibrium audit-effort of good governments, which reduces net revenues and increases inefficiencies.

4.1.2 The static model

We consider two players: a firm i and the government (or its tax authority) g. The sequence of events in the model looks as follows:

1. Nature draws the type of government θ, bad or good. A bad government type θ^b is drawn with probability p, and a good type θ^g with probability $1-p$.

[4]Examples are Marrelli (1984), Wang and Conant (1988), Marrelli and Martina (1988), Virmani (1989), Lee (1998) and Bayer and Cowell (2006). Most of these models are analyzed in Chapter 3.

2. The type is revealed to the government alone.

3. The firm decides whether to evade taxes or not, and the government takes an action penalize or not penalize.

4. The firm and the government receive their payoffs, Π_i and Π_g, respectively.

The following assumptions are made for the model.

1. Both the firm and the government are risk-neutral. Note that risk-neutrality of the agents is a standard assumption in tax evasion games. Moreover, firms are different from individual taxpayers since risk-aversion plays a minor role in firms' behavior. They are more driven by economic incentives.

2. The tax rate t is proportional to the earned profit P, the surcharge on detected tax evasion f is proportional to the amount of evaded tax for the good government. In case of bad government the extortion parameter F is proportional to the firm's profit since the bad government wants to expropriate a certain part of it.

The proportionality of a corporate tax and of penalties on the evaded taxes is quite a common feature of many tax codes. The preferences of the good government are to find and penalize the tax evaders; the bad government penalizes arbitrarily irrespective of the fact whether the firm evades taxes or not since it rather pursues other goals (own benefits, corruption, extortion, or political aims). Consequently, it is not interested in fair taxation. But the extortion parameter F may include some part of evaded taxes or the taxes which the government claims to have been evaded.

3. The costs of investigation incurred by the good government are fixed and equal c whereas the bad government penalizes without any investigation and thus incurs no costs. This assumption seems plausible taking into account the previous argument. In the dynamic game we consider the case when the extortion is connected with costs.

4. The firm is profitable, and the government knows the relative level of the firm's profits. Under this assumption we mean that the government distinguishes between big and small firms being aware of the level of profits they are able to generate. The assumption captures the reality that the government (or its tax authorities) is more inclined to approach and investigate bigger firms[5].

[5]This assumption is mostly relevant for companies in resource sector since prices are dependant on business cycles and thus revenue generating capacity of such firms is quite predictablo.

Since the government and the firm make their decisions simultaneously the government assumes the profitability, for example, in terms of the firm's size while taking the penalization decision. We release this assumption in the next model where the profitability of the firm will be the firm's private information.

4.1.2.1 Payoffs

The ex post payoffs are given below. We start with the government. For the bad and the good government, respectively, they will look as follows:

$$\Pi_g(\theta^b, P) = r[qFP + (1-q)(t+F)P] + (1-r)[(1-q)tP] \tag{4.1}$$

$$\Pi_g(\theta^g, P) = r[q(tP(1+f)-c) + (1-q)(tP-c)] + (1-r)[(1-q)tP], \tag{4.2}$$

where $\Pi_g(\theta^b)$ is the ex post payoff of the bad government, $\Pi_g(\theta^g)$ ex post payoff of the good government, t is the linear tax rate, f the penalty rate on the detected tax evasion, F is the fraction of the profit that can be extorted, P the earned gross profit, c is the investigation costs the good government incurs. q denotes the probability that the firm evades taxes and r is the probability that the firm will be penalized.

From (4.1) we see that for a bad government "penalize" is optimal. Employing tie-breaking rule, the strategy when the bad government is indifferent between its alternatives is not specified, we can summarize the optimal reaction of bad government as

$$r_g^*(\theta^b) = \begin{cases} 1 & if \quad PF > 0 \\ 0 & if \quad PF < 0 \end{cases}$$

For the bad government "penalize" will always be the optimal action under the assumption of firm's profit generating ability ($P > 0$), and if the extortion parameter is positive ($F > 0$).

$$r_g^*(\theta^b) = \{penalize\} \quad \text{for} \quad P > 0$$

The good government's optimal reaction will look as follows:

$$r_g^*(\theta^g) = \begin{cases} 1 & if \quad q > \frac{c}{(1+f)tP} \\ \in [0,1] & if \quad q = \frac{c}{(1+f)tP} \\ 0 & if \quad q < \frac{c}{(1+f)tP} \end{cases}$$

The good government's belief about the firm's evasion will depend on the share of costs in the collected tax revenues. The government will not penalize if the firm doesn't evade and will penalize if the firm evades. The probability of evasion increases with costs of investigation and decreases with the penalty[6].

We now turn to the firm. The corresponding payoff of the firm if it faces the bad government is:

$$\Pi_i(\theta^b, P) = q[r\Pi_e + (1-r)P] + (1-q)[r\Pi_n + (1-r)P(1-t)] \tag{4.3}$$

With the good government the firm's payoff will look as follows:

$$\Pi_i(\theta^g, P) = q[rP(1-t(1+f)) + (1-r)P] + (1-q)[rP(1-t) + (1-r)P(1-t)], \tag{4.4}$$

where Π_e is the firm's payoff if it evades and Π_n is the payoff if the firm does not evade respectively when it faces the bad government[7].

From (4.3) and (4.4) the optimal evasion decision of the firm if it faces the bad and the good government respectively is the following:

$$q_i(\theta^b) = \begin{cases} 1 & if \quad \Pi_e > \Pi_n \\ 0 & if \quad \Pi_e < \Pi_n \end{cases}$$

$$q_i(\theta^g) = \begin{cases} 1 & if \quad r < \frac{1}{1+f} \\ \in [0,1] & if \quad r = \frac{1}{1+f} \\ 0 & if \quad r > \frac{1}{1+f} \end{cases} \tag{4.5}$$

Facing the bad government the firm will evade if the payoff from evasion is more than from non-evasion, and will not evade if the opposite is true. In case of good government the firm evades if it is not penalized and does not evade if it is penalized by the good government.

Higher penalties imposed by the good government presupposes lower audit probability of good government to prevent tax evasion.

We assign probabilities of facing the bad government p which always penalizes, and the good government $1-p$ which mixes between penalization and non-penalization. The firm anticipating the reaction of the two types of governments has the following expected net profits from evasion and compliance respectively:

[6]For the general result see Cowell, F., 1990, p.122.

[7]We characterize equilibria for the general case at first, and then define the firm's payoffs for the case of simple extortion.

$$E\Pi_i(q=1) = p\Pi_e + (1-p)P(1 - r_g^*(\theta^g)t(1+f)) \tag{4.6}$$

$$E\Pi_i(q=0) = p\Pi_n + (1-p)P(1-t) \tag{4.7}$$

In case of evasion (4.6), with the bad government (probability p) the firm gets Π_e, and with the good government (probability $1-p$) the firm realizes the gross earned profit reduced by evaded taxes and penalties weighted at the government's probability of investigation $r_g^*(\theta^g)$.

In case of non-evasion (4.7), with the bad government (probability p) the firm gets Π_n, and with the good government (probability $1-p$) the firm realizes its net profits (gross profits less profit tax).

Comparing these two expected payoffs shows that the optimal evasion decision of the firm will be the following:

1. if $\Pi_e > \Pi_n$
then the optimal evasion decision of the firm in case it is penalized is given by

$$q_i^* = \begin{cases} 0 & if \quad p < Ptf/(\Pi_e - \Pi_n + Ptf)] \\ \in [0;1] & if \quad p = Ptf/(\Pi_e - \Pi_n + Ptf) \\ 1 & if \quad p > Ptf/(\Pi_e - \Pi_n + Ptf) \end{cases}$$

In case of non-penalization the best response of the firm is "evade":

$$q_i^* = 1 \quad \text{for} \quad \forall p$$

If the firm is not penalized it will evade for all levels of p, if it is penalized it will evade for p exceeding a certain level. So that even being penalized the firm has incentives to evade taxes if the probability of bad government is sufficiently high.

2. if $\Pi_e < \Pi_n$
This case can happen if the firm has to pay additional payments which exceed the level of evaded taxes, for example, if tax evasion is connected with high concealment costs.

In case of penalization by the government the best response of the firm is

$$q_i^* = 0 \quad \text{for} \quad \forall p$$

In case of non-penalization the best response is given by

$$q_i^* = \begin{cases} 1 & for \quad p < Pt/(\Pi_n - \Pi_e + Pt) \\ \in [0;1] & for \quad p = Pt/(\Pi_n - \Pi_e + Pt) \\ 0 & for \quad p > Pt/(\Pi_n - \Pi_e + Pt) \end{cases}$$

The firm will not evade if penalized and will evade if p will be less than the certain amount.

The second case is less likely to happen since the firm hardly finds it profitable to evade. Although there is some evidence that Russian firms still evade due to adversary perception of the state. They probably derive some utility from behaving against the state.

In the following we characterize equilibria for both cases, and then derive results based on the first case.

4.1.2.2 Equilibria

To find possible equilibria we need to check the correspondence of the firm's actions with the government's strategies. By inserting in $q = 1$ and $q = 0$ into the government's payoff function we can find the pure strategy equilibria.

- For the case when $\Pi_e > \Pi_n$

1. The pure evasion equilibrium clearly exists whenever

$$c > tP(1 + f),$$

when the costs of investigation are higher than the recovered tax revenues. Being not penalized by the good government $r_g^* = 0$ a firm will always evade taxes $q_i^* = 1$.

2. The equilibrium where being penalized the firm prefers evading taxes exists if

$$p > \frac{Ptf}{\Pi_e - \Pi_n + Ptf}.$$

If the higher probability of facing the bad government is observed the firm finds it optimal to evade taxes, $q_i^* = 1$, since the payoff from evasion will be higher than from non-evasion even if it is penalized by the good government ($r_g^* = 1$).

There is no pure strategy non-evasion equilibrium in case $\Pi_e > \Pi_n$. If the firm does not evade the government prefers not to penalize. If the firm is not penalized it prefers evading. Consequently, there is no pure non-evasion equilibrium.

3. In the hybrid equilibrium, the firm randomizes between evasion and non-evasion. In order to find it we have to find the probability of the government type p which makes the firm indifferent to evasion and compliance.

For the case $\Pi_e > \Pi_n$ equilibrium p equals

$$p = \frac{Ptf}{\Pi_e - \Pi_n + Ptf} \tag{4.8}$$

The good government will be indifferent to its actions if

$q = \frac{c}{(1+f)tP}$.

- For the case when $\Pi_e < \Pi_n$

1. A non-evasion equilibrium will exist for this case when non-evasion is a dominant strategy for the firm. The case when the payoff from evasion will be less than from non-evasion may be if the concealment costs associated with tax evasion are very high.

2. In addition to the non-evasion equilibrium there is an equilibrium where not being penalized by the good government for $c > tP(1+f)$ the firm will evade taxes if the probability of facing bad government is sufficiently small so that

$$p < \frac{Pt}{\Pi_n - \Pi_e + Pt}.$$

3. For the second case when $\Pi_e < \Pi_n$ the probability p in equilibrium will equal

$$p = \frac{Pt}{\Pi_n - \Pi_e + Pt}, \tag{4.9}$$

when the firm will be indifferent between evasion and compliance. The

good government will be indifferent to its actions if
$q = \frac{c}{(1+f)tP}$.

We consider the first case when the profit from evasion is more than from non-evasion if the firm faces bad government. This case is more likely to happen. That's mostly exacerbates tax evasion incentives. We consider extortion on the side of the bad government.

Under extortion we assume that the firm is penalized arbitrarily by the bad government with the extortion parameter F on its profits P. The case corresponds to the situation when the government (or its tax authority) extorts money from the firm, irrespective whether it evaded taxes or not.

The firm's expected net profits from evasion (4.6) and non-evasion (4.7) will be modified as follows

$$E\Pi_i(q=1) = pP(1-F) + (1-p)P(1-r_g^*(\theta^g)t(1+f)) \tag{4.10}$$

$$E\Pi_i(q=0) = pP(1-t-F) + (1-p)P(1-t) \tag{4.11}$$

The equilibrium belief about the government type will be $p = \frac{f}{1+f}$. For this level of probability of facing bad government p the firm will be indifferent to evasion and compliance.

Proposition 1. *In the presence of uncertainty about the government type (good or bad) and in case of extortion from the bad type, the equilibrium belief about the government type p when the firm mixes between evasion and non-evasion depends solely on the penalties the good government imposes on tax evaders f.*

The firm's optimal evasion decision depending on its belief about the good government's penalization will be the following

$$q_i^* = \begin{cases} 1 & if \quad r_g^* < \frac{1}{(1-p)(1+f)} \\ 0 & if \quad r_g^* > \frac{1}{(1-p)(1+f)} \end{cases} \tag{4.12}$$

Compare this with the optimal evasion decision of the firm when only one good type of government is taken into account (4.5). The probability of facing bad government alleviates the penalties' deterrent effect. The higher probability p, the higher penalties the good government should apply to be able to deter tax evasion under the given probability of penalization.

Figure 4.1 shows the dependence of the equilibrium type on the level of penalties. If the firm is not penalized it prefers evading for all p, since evasion pays with certainty. Knowing this the government tries to increase investigation and to penalize the firm. If the government penalizes evading turns not optimal. The equilibrium switches to hybrid where the firm mixes between evasion and non-evasion.

With a higher p evasion becomes more optimal for the firm. With the penalties normally applied for tax evasion the equilibrium switches from hybrid to pure evasion again.

Proposition 2. *The higher the probability of facing bad government the higher the level of tax evasion.*

Figure 4.1: Effect of the equilibrium probability of government's type p on penalties for tax evasion f

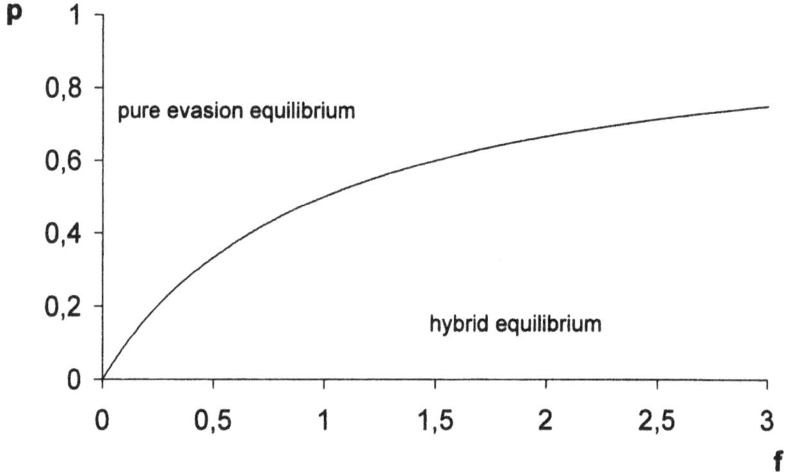

Proof. We need to show that the higher belief of facing the bad government p is associated with higher penalties for tax evasion imposed by the good government. A rise in the penalty rate for evasion increases the firm's belief of facing bad government in equilibrium.

$\partial p/\partial f = \frac{1}{(1+f)^2} > \frac{f}{1+f}$.

Since $f \neq -1$, the derivative exists and is certainly positive. Moreover, as the level of penalties in the equilibrium condition for playing hybrid remains unchanged, it means that for some p the firm changes from hybrid to the pure evasion equilibrium ($\frac{1}{(1+f)^2} > \frac{f}{1+f}$). Consequently, if the probability that the government is bad is high, it may cause a rise in tax evasion.

For example, consider the case where the firm has high perception that the government is bad due to its extortive activities, as can be the case in developing and transition economies. With the penalties applied for tax evasion (normally 15-20 percent of the evaded taxes) the situation corresponds to the pure evasion equilibrium (upper left region of the figure 4.1). This can also partly explain the high levels of tax evasion in some economies.

Very high penalties are needed to deter tax evasion if the probability of bad government is high, but in practice penalties are not advised to be set too high. Thus it is argued that tax evasion can not be treated as other crimes not deserving very severe punishment. Depending on the probability of a bad government and taking into account that the penalties can not be set too high, their increase is also limited by the certain level. Consequently, with the high prior probability of bad government the level of tax evasion is expected to be higher.

The firm's perception about facing the bad government in equilibrium does not depend on the arbitrarily applied extortion parameter F, e.g. on the level of money being extorted, but on penalties imposed on tax evaders by the good government f. Consequently, to bring tax evasion down penalties for tax evasion should not be increased, but extortion should be limited.

Figure 4.2: Effect of the income parameter P on penalties for tax evasion f

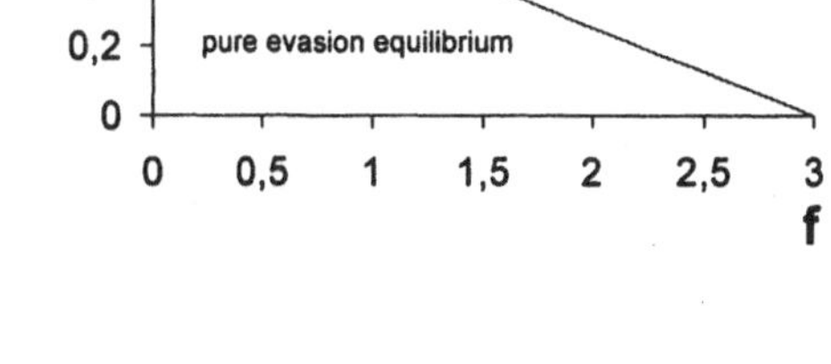

Figure 4.2 illustrates how the firm's profit depends on the penalties for tax evasion[8]. Higher penalties for evasion reduce the firm's profit P. The pure evasion equilibrium is observed with lower penalties and higher profits.

[8]The parameter settings were P=1, t=0,25.

If the firm evades taxes it can bribe a politician in order to escape extortion. To make it profitable for the firm the bribe should be less than the extortion parameter. Also with increasing penalties, the level of bribes normally increases as the politician requires a larger share to be able to hide evasion.

Proposition 3. *Tax evasion incentives are increased if bribery is possible to escape extortion.*

Proof. The firm's payoffs when it evades and does not evade with the bad government, but can bribe in case of evasion will look as follows:

$\Pi_e = P(1-b)$
$\Pi_n = P(1-t-F)$, where b is bribe.

The new equilibrium belief about the government type is

$$p = \frac{tf}{t(1+f)+(F-b)} \tag{4.13}$$

which will make sense only if $F-b$ is positive. Moreover, as f rises $(F-b)$ will fall.

The bribe decreases the equilibrium belief p about the government type.

$$p = \frac{tf}{t(1+f)+(F-b)} < \frac{f}{1+f} \tag{4.14}$$

The evasion starts to pay even for lower levels of p. Consequently, bribery intensifies tax evasion. Extortion may lead to the fact that firms will prefer to bribe to escape it.

Figure 4.3 illustrates the equilibrium path with the increasing tax rate. As tax rate rises, evasion pays more (in the pure evasion equilibrium), but the evasion decision is not influenced by the increase of the tax rate in the hybrid equilibrium. Even for small p, tax evasion may increase. This result is compatible with a lot of models which say that the higher tax rates induce more evasion. It is also consistent with the reality observed at the beginning of transition in Russia. Thus, setting of high and numerous taxes resulted in a significant increase of tax evasion.

4.1.3 The dynamic game

In this model we relax the assumption about the profitability of the firm, now it will become the firm's private information. A firm decides on its profit

Figure 4.3: Effect of the income parameter P on tax rate t

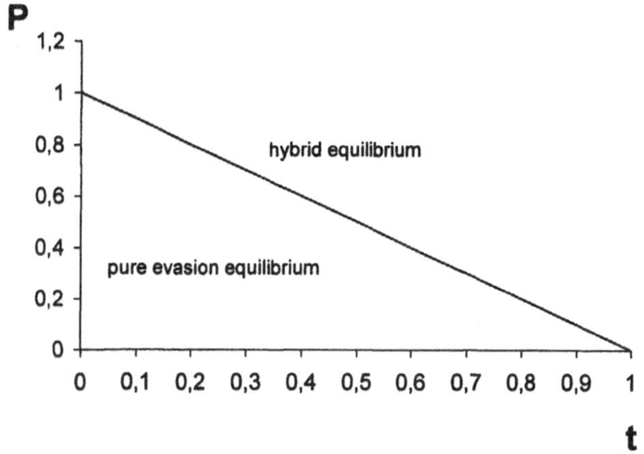

declaration for tax purposes, while being uncertain about the objective of the government. The government takes its actions after observing the firm's declaration of profits.

We find that the prior probability of facing an extortionist government increases tax evasion incentives. The firm will evade taxes even if it is always audited by the good government due to a certain likelihood of facing a bad government which extorts. Therefore the potential for extortion undermines revenue collection of good governments. Moreover, the prior probability of firms facing a bad government increases the expected equilibrium audit-effort of good governments, which reduces net revenue and increases inefficiencies.

Consider again two players: a firm i and the government (or its tax authority) g.

The firm may be profitable or not. This is information private to the firm. The gross profit may be $\rho \in \{0, \pi\}$, with $\lambda \in (0, 1)$ denoting the commonly known prior probability for $\rho = \pi$.

The government may by of type $\theta^g = 0$ (a well-meaning good government) or of type $\theta^b = 1$ (a malicious extortive government). The prior probability for a bad government $\theta = \theta^b$ is denoted by $p \in (0, 1)$.

The sequence of events in the model looks as follows:

1. Nature independently draws the types of firm and government.

2. Both players learn their own types.

3. The firm declares its profit $d_i \in \{0, \pi\}$.

4. The government observes d_i and takes an action $a_g \in \{nothing; audit; extort\}$.

5. The payoffs are realized.

4.1.3.1 Payoffs

Now we will define the ex-post payoffs. We start with the firm

$$\Pi_i(\rho, d_i, a_g) := \begin{cases} \rho - td_i & if \quad a_g = nothing \\ \rho - td_i - t(1+f)\max\{0, \rho - d_i\} & if \quad a_g = audit \\ \rho - \rho F - td_i & if \quad a_g = extort \end{cases} \tag{4.15}$$

where t is the (linear) tax rate, f is the penalty rate on detected tax evasion, and F denotes the fraction of profit that can be extorted.

If the firm is not investigated, it will pay taxes only on its declared profits td_i; being audited, the firm has additionally to pay non-declared taxes and penalties on them. If extortion takes place, additionally to the declared taxes the firm pays the fraction of its profits as extortion money ρF.

The ex-post payoff of the government is defined as:

$$\Pi_g(\theta, a_g, d_i, \rho) := \begin{cases} td_i & if \quad a_g = nothing \\ td_i + t(1+f)\max\{0, \rho - d_i\} - c & if \quad a_g = audit \\ td_i + \rho F - C(\theta) & if \quad a_g = extort \end{cases} . \tag{4.16}$$

Here c denotes the audit cost, while $C(\theta)$ denotes the moral cost a government has to bear whenever it extorts. This cost can be interpreted as the sum of transaction, bribery and reputation cost arising from extortion. We assume $C(\theta^g) = \infty$ and $C(\theta^b) = 0$ to ensure that a good government does not want to extort, while a bad government has no scruples to do so. Additionally, we assume that gross revenues from extortion exceed those from punishing an evading firm:

$$F > t(1+f) \tag{4.17}$$

We need to explain how extortion works and why we get the payoff that we assume. Suppose a government that tries to extort contacts the firm and threatens to expropriate the firm and/or to imprison the managers if the firm does not co-operate. Then F could be seen as a parameter determined by the relative bargaining power of the government, which is highly skewed toward the government. The fraction of profit that can be extorted F in reality depends on the degree of control the government has over courts and enforcement agencies. A tighter grip increases the fraction of profit that can be extorted.[9]

4.1.3.2 Solving the game

We have a dynamic game of incomplete information. We use Perfect Bayesian Nash Equilibrium PBE as a solution concept. We see - by using equations (4.16) and (4.17) - that for a bad government auditing is a dominated strategy. Extortion always pays for a bad government:

$$a_g^*(\theta^b, d_i) = \{extort\} \quad \text{for} \quad d_i \in \{0, \pi\}. \tag{4.18}$$

A good government does not want to extort, since the extortion costs are unbearably high for the good government. But it has to decide whether to audit or not. Given that a good government observes a declaration of π it is a dominant strategy not to audit, as no fines would ever be collected after an audit:

$$a_g^*(\theta^g, d_i = \pi) = \{nothing\}. \tag{4.19}$$

We now turn to the case where a good government observes a zero declaration. The decision of the government (or tax authority) depends on the believed probability that a zero declaration comes from a profitable firm. We denote this belief by

$$\mu = prob(\rho = \pi | d_i = 0). \tag{4.20}$$

Observing that it is a dominant strategy for a firm with $\rho = 0$ to declare $d_i = 0$ (it never pays for a firm to declare a profit if it is not profitable) we can use Bayes' rule to determine a correct belief. Denote the equilibrium probability that a profitable firm declares no profit (the probability of tax evasion) as q^*, we have

[9]However, given this interpretation we probably would need some extortion cost $C(\theta^b) > 0$ arising from the bargaining and the effort of finding out how much the government has earned. Then we get an additional complication as there are parameter values under which the bad government prefers to do nothing to extortion.

$$\mu = \frac{\lambda q^*}{\lambda q^* + 1 - \lambda}. \tag{4.21}$$

Then a good authority audits whenever

$$\begin{aligned} \mu t(1+f)\pi - c &> 0, \quad \text{or inserting (4.21) and rearranging we get} \\ q_i^* &> \frac{c(1-\lambda)}{\lambda\left(\pi t\left(1+f\right)-c\right)}. \end{aligned}$$

The good government will audit if the audit costs will be less than tax revenues with penalties recovered from the evading firm weighted at the government belief about firm's tax evasion.

Denoting the equilibrium audit probability of a good government after an observation of $d_i = 0$ as r_g^* we summarize the optimal reaction as:

$$r_g^* = \begin{cases} 1 & if \quad q_i^* > \frac{c(1-\lambda)}{\lambda(\pi t(1+f)-c)} \\ 0 & if \quad q_i^* < \frac{c(1-\lambda)}{\lambda(\pi t(1+f)-c)} \end{cases} \tag{4.22}$$

The good government will audit if the firm is believed to evade taxes, and will not do it if the firm does not evade. Since the strategy is not specified when the government is indifferent between auditing and doing nothing (playing a mixed strategy), we can use a tie-breaking rule.

We now turn to the firm. As mentioned above it is a dominant strategy for a firm which is not profitable to declare no profit. So

$$d_i^*(\rho = 0) = 0. \tag{4.23}$$

A firm anticipating the reaction of the two types of governments has the following expected net profits from evasion and compliance:

$$E\Pi_i(d_i = 0|\rho = \pi) = \pi\left(1 - pF - (1-p)\, r_g^* t\,(1+f)\right) \tag{4.24}$$

$$E\Pi_i(d_i = \pi|\rho = \pi) = \pi(1 - t - pF). \tag{4.25}$$

Comparing these two expected payoffs shows that the optimal evasion decision is as follows:

$$q_i^* = \begin{cases} 1 & if \quad r_g^* < \frac{1}{(1-p)(1+f)} \\ \in [0,1] & if \quad r_g^* = \frac{1}{(1-p)(1+f)} \\ 0 & if \quad r_g^* > \frac{1}{(1-p)(1+f)} \end{cases} \tag{4.26}$$

The result which we derived in the static framework holds (see 4.12). We see that the higher the probability of facing a bad government, the higher the probability of an audit by the good government has to be to prevent evasion. The higher the penalties on tax evasion, the lower the probability of an audit of the good government has to be to prevent evasion.

4.1.3.3 Equilibria

We can now characterize the equilibria arising from different parameter settings.

1. The surrender-to-evasion equilibrium. If

$$\frac{c(1-\lambda)}{\lambda\left(\pi t\left(1+f\right)-c\right)}>1 \tag{4.27}$$

then a good government will never audit $r_g^*=0$, and a profitable firm will always evade $q_i^*=1$ as $0<1/\left[(1-p)(1+f)\right]$.

2. The audit-evasion equilibrium. If

$$\begin{aligned}\frac{c(1-\lambda)}{\lambda\left(\pi t\left(1+f\right)-c\right)} &< 1 \quad \text{and} \\ \frac{1}{(1-p)(1+f)} &> 1\end{aligned}$$

then a profitable firm will always evade $q_i^*=1$, even though a good government will audit all zero declarations $r_g^*=1$. The driving force behind this equilibrium is probability of facing a bad government. Then it pays to evade because the payoff will be higher under evasion if extortion takes place.

3. The mixed-evasion equilibrium. If

$$\begin{aligned}\frac{c(1-\lambda)}{\lambda\left(\pi t\left(1+f\right)-c\right)} &\leq 1 \quad \text{and} \\ \frac{1}{(1-p)(1+f)} &\leq 1\end{aligned}$$

then both the profitable firm and the good government will mix. Given that both must be indifferent between their possible actions we have

$$\begin{aligned} r_g^* &= \frac{1}{(1-p)(1+f)} \quad \text{and} \\ q_i^* &= \frac{c(1-\lambda)}{\lambda\left(\pi t\left(1+f\right)-c\right)}. \end{aligned}$$

These results shows that the deterrent effect of audits are diminished. Moreover, with a high probability of a bad government the effect of audits on tax evasion may even be neglected as the firm will continue evading.

The good government may try to increase penalties. But depending on the probability of a bad government and taking into account that the penalties can not be set too high, their increase is also limited by the certain level. Under given probability of audits r^* the increase of penalties may not have a strong impact on deterring tax evasion if the probability of bad government is high.

Proposition 4. *The deterrent effect of penalties and audits imposed on tax evaders by the good government is diminished if the probability of facing an extortionist government is high.*

4.1.3.4 Costly extortion

If there are positive extortion costs $C(\theta^b) > 0$ (see the footnote 9) then the whole story gets a bit different. The decision to extort or not for a bad government becomes dependent on parameters and on the declaration strategy.

Define $\theta^b = 1$ and $\theta^g = 0$. Redefine the payoff of the government from eq. (4.16) as

$$\Pi_g(\theta, a_g, d_i, \rho) := \begin{cases} td_i & if \quad a_g = nothing \\ td_i + t(1+f)\max\{0, \rho - d_i\} - c & if \quad a_g = audit \\ td_i + \rho F - \frac{cK}{\theta} & if \quad a_g = extort \end{cases} \tag{4.28}$$

For the good government the extortion cost goes to $-\infty$, while for a bad government the extortion cost are cK. These costs can be interpreted as the sum of transaction, bribery, and reputation costs arising from extortion. For example, bad governments often do not care about building good reputations having low horizons. So that their reputation costs are low.

We assume that $K < 1$, which means extortion is less costly than an audit. Then auditing remains a dominated strategy for a bad government. The condition for an audit of the good government is still the same. However, the decision of the bad government changes. Given that a firm with $\rho = 0$ never declares any income, the governments know that a declaration of π comes from a profitable firm. Therefore in case of a declaration $d_i = \pi$, extortion always pays for a bad government

$$a_g^*(\theta^b, d_i = \pi) = \{extort\}. \tag{4.29}$$

Whether a bad government tries to extort if a zero declaration is observed, or just does nothing, depends on the belief that the firm's true profit is π. Denoting this belief as μ the condition for extortion becomes:

$$\mu F\pi - cK \geq 0. \tag{4.30}$$

Extortion money weighted at the believed probability of evasion has to be more than the incurred extortion costs cK.

Using the definition of μ from eq. (4.21) we can define the critical evasion-probability. Then the sequentially rational response of a bad government (where σ denotes the probability of extortion) can be given as:

$$\sigma_g^* = \begin{cases} 1 \;\; if \;\; q_i^* > \frac{cK(1-\lambda)}{(F\pi - cK)\lambda} \\ 0 \;\; if \;\; q_i^* < \frac{cK(1-\lambda)}{(F\pi - cK)\lambda} \end{cases} \tag{4.31}$$

The extortion decision of a bad government will depend in this case on the extortion costs. High extortion costs presuppose higher critical evasion probability q_i^* for a bad government to start to extort. Consequently, if reputation, transaction costs arising from extortion are low, and the government controls courts and enforcement agencies, thus being able to extort higher fraction of profits, a very small probability of tax evasion is necessary in order for a bad government to extort. We now have to modify the condition for profitable evasion from eq. 4.24, 4.25:

$$E\Pi_i(d_i = 0|\rho = \pi) = \pi\left(1 - p\sigma_g^* F - (1-p)\, r_g^* t\,(1+f)\right) \tag{4.32}$$

$$E\Pi_i(d_i = \pi|\rho = \pi) = \pi(1 - t - pF). \tag{4.33}$$

The evasion condition becomes

$$r_g^* < \frac{pF(1-\sigma_g^*) + t}{(1-p)t(1+f)}. \tag{4.34}$$

High probability of a bad government p and the fraction of extorted profits F increase tax evasion incentives to the firm and offset the enforcement efforts of the good government.

4.1.3.5 Equilibria

Different partitions in the parameter space lead to different equilibria. One equilibrium we can rule out is the totally mixed equilibrium. It is easy to see that for any parameter configuration $\sigma_g^* \geq r_g^*$ holds. The reason is simple. The critical evasion probability for extortion (by a bad government)(4.31) is smaller than that for audits (by a good government)(4.22).

$$\frac{cK(1-\lambda)}{(F\pi - cK)\lambda} < \frac{c(1-\lambda)}{\lambda(\pi t(1+f)-c)}$$

Therefore there is no totally mixed equilibrium, as an evasion probability that makes the good government indifferent induces extortion.

Possible equilibria are:

1. The surrender-to-evasion equilibrium. If

$$\frac{c(1-\lambda)}{\lambda(\pi t(1+f)-c)} > 1 \tag{4.35}$$

then a good government will never audit $r_g^* = 0$, and a profitable firm will always evade $q_i^* = 1$ as $0 < \left[t + pF(1-\sigma_g^*)\right] / \left[(1-p)t(1+f)\right]$ $\forall \sigma_g^* \in [0,1]$. Extortion is possible in this equilibrium. Using eq. (4.31) there will be extortion whenever

$$\frac{cK(1-\lambda)}{(F\pi - cK)\lambda} \leq 1 \tag{4.36}$$

Lower extortion costs and higher level of profits which can be extorted make extortion more probable.

2. The audit-evasion equilibrium. If

$$\begin{aligned} \frac{c(1-\lambda)}{\lambda(\pi t(1+f)-c)} &< 1 \quad \text{and} \\ \frac{1}{(1-p)(1+f)} &> 1 \end{aligned}$$

then a profitable firm will always evade $q_i^* = 1$, even though a good government will audit all zero declarations $r_g^* = 1$. The driving force behind this equilibrium is a high probability of facing a bad government. Then it pays to evade because the payoff will be higher under evasion if extortion takes place. Note that the second condition comes from eq. (4.34) with $\sigma_g^* = 1$, as if audits are profitable for good governments then extortion is profitable for bad governments. Note that there is a critical $p > 0$ needed for this equilibrium to exist. Therefore evasion when audits are certain is only an equilibrium if the prior probability for a bad government is sufficiently large. This is intuitively clear. A firm which understands that it will always be audited by a good government, only evades if there is a certain likelihood of facing a bad government. Then evasion is better than honesty given that extortion will take place.

This finding explain why in spite of auditing evasion is still a big problem for countries with bad governments.

Proposition 5. *If the probability of facing an extortionist government is high, a firm may evade taxes even if a good government audits with certainty and there are positive extortion costs.*

3. Full-extortion mixed-evasion equilibrium. If

$$\frac{c(1-\lambda)}{\lambda\left(\pi t\left(1+f\right)-c\right)} \leq 1 \quad \text{and}$$
$$\frac{1}{(1-p)(1+f)} \leq 1$$

then both the profitable firm and the good government will mix. Given that then both must be indifferent to their possible actions we have

$$\begin{aligned} r_g^* &= \frac{1}{(1-p)(1+f)}, \\ q_i^* &= \frac{c(1-\lambda)}{\lambda\left(\pi t\left(1+f\right)-c\right)} \quad \text{and} \\ \sigma_g^* &= 1. \end{aligned}$$

The bad government will always extort in this equilibrium. In this equilibrium an increasing prior probability of bad government increases the auditing effort of good government ($dr_g^*/dp > 0$).

The presence of bad governments provides incentives for higher evasion, which induces good governments to audit more frequently in order to keep the firm indifferent between evasion and truthful declaration. Therefore the presence of bad governments increases the expected audit cost and thus produces higher welfare losses.

The expected welfare loss for a good government, measured as its expected audit cost, is given by

$$E(c|\theta=0) = \frac{c}{(1-p)(1+f)}[(1-\lambda) + \frac{c(1-\lambda)\lambda}{\lambda\left(\pi t\left(1+f\right)-c\right)}] \qquad (4.37)$$

which increases with the probability of facing a bad government. Note that only the bad governments make an expected profit in equilibrium.

> The reaction of the good government to changes in the environment (i.e. the adjustment of the audit probability) makes extortion always profitable. This shows how the potential existence of bad governments makes life difficult for good governments.

Summing up, the following conclusions can be made:

1. If there are two government types - good, which is interested in curbing tax evasion, and bad, which is prone to extortion - the higher the probability of bad government the higher the level of tax evasion.
2. When extortion by a bad government takes place the probability of bad government in equilibrium does not depend on the extortion parameter (the fraction of profits being extorted) but on the penalties the good government imposes on tax evaders. With a high probability of facing bad government and penalties normally applied, the situation corresponds to the pure evasion equilibrium. The deterrent effect of penalties is thus alleviated.
3. Bribery intensifies tax evasion. The equilibrium probability of a bad government decreases if a firm can offer bribes. Evasion starts to pay for a lower probability of facing the bad government.
4. If the tax rate rises, tax evasion increases, but the probability of a bad government does not influence the evasion decision of the firm.
5. If the probability of facing a bad government is high the firm will evade taxes even though being audited by a good government is certain. Consequently, the deterrent effect of audits as well as the effect of penalties can be alleviated in this case. With sufficiently high probability of facing the bad government the audit-evasion equilibrium is observed. The result also holds if extortion is costly for the bad government.
6. The presence of bad government will increase the expected audit costs of good governments. The expected welfare loss for a good government will rise with the probability of bad government.
7. Consequently, curbing extortion will be an important step to increase tax compliance among companies and reduce expenditure on tax enforcement.

We have considered the corporate tax evasion induced by the bad government behavior such as extortion. We have proved how this cause may influence evasion decision of firms and affect adversely tax policy parameters used by the good government to deter evasion.

The deterrent effect of penalties and audits is distorted if probability of bad government is high. Thus being audited with certainty by the good government a firm will find it optimal to evade taxes if the probability of facing an extortionist government is high. Revenue collection of good governments is undermined if there is potential for extortion. Consequently, combatting extortion is an important step to reduce the evasion level in the economy.

On the other side, firms themselves are actively engaged in implementation of different evading techniques which we analyzed in the second chapter. So that apart from evasion induced by bad government corporate tax evasion methods should be considered. The most widely used tax evasion technique is the practice when firms manipulate their expenses and profits. They understate profits and labor costs as tax bases and overstate other costs diminishing profit and VAT tax bases.

In the following we analyze how distortion of financial data takes place by tax evasion and the effects of tax policy parameters to deter this incentive. We also propose a tax regime which may potentially alleviate this incentive of firms to engage in expenses and profit manipulation and at the same time decrease government discretion.

4.2 Mechanism to restrain tax evasion incentives

4.2.1 Corporate tax evasion techniques

Having considered the causes of tax evasion and how, for example, extortion may influence corporate tax evasion and policy parameters, in the following we focus on corporate evasion techniques which enable us to derive the tax policy design in order to reduce the evasion level in the Russian economy.

To analyze tax evasion techniques formally we employ the framework proposed by Yakovlev, A. (2001) who investigated black cash tax evasion. Black cash tax evasion is a well-known form of tax evasion in Russia which was especially widespread in the nineties. That is because cash transactions are widely used in Russia that eases opportunities to evade. If a firm receives cash it is easier to evade taxes by paying out salaries and profits without registering these transactions. That is why the form is known as black or unregistered cash tax evasion. Banks also helps firms to implement this kind of evasion by providing them with cash.

The empirical finding of Yakovlev is that the main incentive to evade taxes implies excessive taxation and an unfair tax system. The state does nothing for business and workers in exchange for tax payments. In terms of tax policy he proposes presumptive taxation[10]. Presumptive taxation involves the use of

[10]See Yakovlev, A., 2001.

indirect means to ascertain tax liability, such as, for example, reconstructing income based on administrative practice[11].

Yakovlev assumes that there is a competitive market and that labor taxes are withholding. It means that there are no pure profits and employers are responsible for paying income and social security contributions of employees. Then the revenues of a firm will look as follows

$$V = C + L + I + T, \tag{4.38}$$

where V total revenues, C costs of goods, L labor costs, I capital income (after-tax normal profit of the firm), T total taxes or income of the state.

T can be considered as a function of C, L and I; $T = f(C, L, I)$. As taxes in Russia are mainly proportional the function will take the following form

$$T = \alpha_1 C + \alpha_2 L + \alpha_3 I \tag{4.39}$$

where $\alpha_1, \alpha_2, \alpha_3$ are tax rates on expenses (the sum of VAT levied on intermediate inputs), labor and profit respectively.

For simplicity other taxes (property tax, license payments, etc.) are omitted.

Substituting (4.39) into (4.38) we get

$$V = C(1 + \alpha_1) + L(1 + \alpha_2) + I(1 + \alpha_3). \tag{4.40}$$

Since $\alpha_1, \alpha_2, \alpha_3$ are exogenously given, the tax evader normally manipulates C, L and I to obtain their distorted values C', L' and I' and so to pay less taxes T'. With tax evasion (4.38) will look as follows

$$V' = C' + L' + I' + T' \tag{4.41}$$

Under condition that $V = V'$[12] we will have from (4.40) and (4.41):

$$C(1 + \alpha_1) + L(1 + \alpha_2) + I(1 + \alpha_3) = C' + L' + I' + T'. \tag{4.42}$$

In reality the firm pays out a part of labor and capital income in the legal form, the rest is hidden and proceeds in cash.

$$L = L' + L_c \quad and \quad I = I' + I_c, \tag{4.43}$$

[11] Thuronyi, V., Presumptive taxation, in: Tax law design and drafting, vol.1, IMF, 1996.

[12] The firm will get the same amount of revenues ($V = V'$) but will manipulate with its components.

so that real labor costs and profit consist of reported values which are distorted L' and I' and values which are hidden in cash L_c and I_c. Inserting into (4.42) we have

$$C(1+\alpha_1) + L'\alpha_2 + L_c(1+\alpha_2) + I'\alpha_3 + I_c(1+\alpha_3) = C' + T'.$$

Substituting T' for $\alpha_1 C' + \alpha_2 L' + \alpha_3 I'$

$$C(1+\alpha_1) + L_c(1+\alpha_2) + I_c(1+\alpha_3) = C'(1+\alpha_1), \tag{4.44}$$

and simplifying we will get

$$L_c(1+\alpha_2) + I_c(1+\alpha_3) = (1+\alpha_1)(C' - C). \tag{4.45}$$

At least in the short-run the firm is able to get an additional profit from evasion π. The evading firm will also be interested in L' and $I' \to 0$ trying to underreport as much of them as it can and $C' \to C' + L' + I'$ trying to overreport. So that the difference between the distorted costs C' and real costs C will be the fictitious costs C_f $(C' - C = C_f)$.

$$L = L' + L_c \to L' < L \qquad I = I' + I_c + \pi \to I' < I \qquad C' = C + C_f \to C' > C \tag{4.46}$$

The firm will try to substitute $L_c + I_c + \pi$ for C_f, incurring some concealment costs c. The firm will replace the hidden cash from profits and labor costs as well as profit for tax evasion for other costs which are deductible from the profit tax base.

$$C_f = (1+c)(L_c + I_c + \pi). \tag{4.47}$$

Inserting C_f from (4.47) into (4.45) we will get

$$L_c(1+\alpha_2) + I_c(1+\alpha_3) = (1+\alpha_1)(1+c)(L_c + I_c + \pi). \tag{4.48}$$

$$L_c + I_c + \pi = \frac{L_c(1+\alpha_2) + I_c(1+\alpha_3)}{(1+\alpha_1)(1+c)}. \tag{4.49}$$

After some rearrangements profit from tax evasion π can be defined as follows:

$$\pi = \frac{L_c(\alpha_2 - \alpha_1 - c(1+\alpha_1)) + I_c(\alpha_3 - \alpha_1 - c(1+\alpha_1))}{(1+\alpha_1)(1+c)}. \tag{4.50}$$

As the amount of hidden profits and labor costs I_c and L_c are chosen by the firm, apart from increasing concealment costs c, the state could concentrate on setting tax rates $(\alpha_1, \alpha_2, \alpha_3)$ so that the level of profit from evasion π will be reduced.

The simple way is to reduce labor taxes α_2 (mainly social security contributions) and profit tax α_3, and to increase production taxes α_1, for example VAT. Whereas the reduction of labor taxes may have a positive impact on true reporting of labor costs, profit tax is a more complicated issue. For example, profit tax contains production taxes, so its decrease does not necessarily bring about the desired effect concerning hidden profits[13],[14].

The concealment of labor costs appears to be a big problem since there are employees who suffer from this employers' evading activity. With the transition to saving pension accounts they lose part of their future pensions they would get if they were paid the whole sum of their wages legally. Moreover, with payroll and individual income taxes evaded, the social sphere has trouble fighting poverty.

As for hidden profits, they are considered as pure profits at firms whose evasion is the result of expenses and revenues manipulation, i.e. the overstatement of the first and the understatement of the second.

As can be seen from (4.50) apart from tax rates $\alpha_1, \alpha_2, \alpha_3$ and concealment costs c which the government can influence directly through standard tax policy instruments there are also two variables L_c and I_c which are chosen by the firm, but which have to be minimized in order to lower tax evasion. As it was proven by empirical studies and observed evidence the decrease of income, social security and profit tax contributed only to the small extent to the decrease of evaded tax bases. For example, the increased tax base of payroll taxes was more influenced by increased wages[15].

Firms still have an incentive to distort their profits and expenses concealing some part of them. In order to alleviate this incentive we propose a tax regime which will pose an incentive for firms to report true values of profits I and labor costs L.

---

[13] See Yakovlev, A., 2001

[14] As a result of tax reform, profit and labor taxes have been already substantially reduced. Russian firms still conceal some part of profits and payroll in spite of labor and profit tax reduction.

[15] See Vasiljeva, A., Gurvich, E., 2004.

4.2.2 Tax regime in the presence of tax evasion

4.2.2.1 Problem's description and theory

When analyzing tax evasion a typical problem arises: firms (individuals) hold private information on their tax-paying abilities and will not report them truthfully unless the government ("principal") gives the "agents" an incentive to do so. As it was highlighted above, firms normally have an incentive to misrepresent their expenses in order to manipulate the final outcome (profit). The lack of sufficient information makes it necessary for the government to search for means to achieve certain social goals.

As we have already shown in paragraph 4.1 frequent audits and higher penalties may not produce the desired effect of tax evasion reduction or the deterrent effect of these instruments may be alleviated. The existence of bad governments increases the level of tax evasion in a particular economy. Thus, the bad government's existence may alleviate the good government's auditing efforts and penalties' deterrent effect. The higher the probability of bad government the less efficient the good governments' audits and penalties may be, so that even stricter, more coercive measures are needed to deter firms from evasion.

In the last years some alternative mechanisms were discussed and implemented to increase tax compliance among companies. The proposals varied from liberalization and simplification of tax rules to presumptive taxation. The latter is based on the calculation of company income according to observable characteristics. Moreover, in 2001 the Russian government discussed the possibility of tax liability assessments. The method concerns monitoring expenditures that would allow tax authorities to accrue extra income tax on taxpayer's income on the basis of such expenditures[16]. With this proposal they would try to alleviate corporate incentive to overstate expenses.

It still appears to be difficult to find an empirical model which captures the relationships between observables that accounts for the influence of unobservables[17]. In case of personal income such an indirect method can be seen in identifying the gap between income and expenditure at the aggregate level. In case of firms those observables should be identified which likely correlate with profit. Bond and Devereux (2003) proposed some kind of cash flow tax with minimum information requirements for tax authorities to implement this tax. All the information tax organs should have access to are cash inflows from the real activity of a firm[18].

[16]See Makedonskiy, S., 2005, p.39.

[17]See Cowell, F., 2003, p.7.

[18]See Bond, S.R., Devereux, M.P., 2003, p.1303.

We propose an alternative mechanism which allows to calculate profits and taxes on the basis of costs (the share of labor costs in the total costs). When evading, firms try to reduce the amount of labor costs (thus evading social security contributions and individual income tax) and potentially overstate the amount of other costs (VAT evasion). Due to this substitution the share of labor costs of the total costs is drastically diminished, and firms' profits which are subject to profit tax are also reduced. The mechanism designed by the government should make firms report costs truthfully. They should eventually select the very outcome that the principal (government) considers desirable a priori.

The problem can be potentially described as a mechanism design problem where the firms' ability to evade taxes (firms' types) is their private information.

The sequence of events will look as follows:

Stage 1: The government designs an incentive scheme, where firms send costless messages. Depending on these messages the allocation is chosen by the government.

Stage 2: The firms simultaneously accept or reject the mechanism.

Stage 3: The firms which accept the mechanism play the game specified by the mechanism.

It should be in the interest of firms to accept the mechanism and announce truthfully at stages 2 and 3. But usually if the government acts as a principal the stage 2 can be omitted. Stage 2 presupposes the individual-rationality constraint (IR), that firms will be willing to participate in the mechanism. In our case an IR constraint is not imposed. The state can just set up the mechanism.

Consider the following environment:

1. There are two players, the firm and the government (principal).

2. The set of outcomes is given by I.

3. The firm has private information about its type $\theta \in [\underline{\theta}; \overline{\theta}]$. The set of possible types for the firm varies from non-evaders' type $\underline{\theta}$ to high evaders' type $\overline{\theta}$ (from those who do not evade to complete evaders).

4. The utility function of the firm with the profits as its argument is $u(I, \theta)$, where the firm is of type θ and its profit is I.

5. Suppose that if the government knew the firm's evasion level (type θ) it would choose an outcome in I specified by the social choice function $f(\theta)$.

6. Since the government does not know the firm's evasion level it can only rely on "messages" collected from the firm. These messages are reporting of costs (share of labor costs in the total costs) which express the types (the firm's evasion level). Let L/C_t denote the set of all messages the firm could send. If, for example, θ is the firm's evasion ability (the misreporting of costs and profits reflects this ability) then $\frac{L}{C_t}(\overline{\theta})$ is the message from an evading firm.

7. A mechanism is a message space L/C_t and a decision rule g, which forces an outcome in I for each message profile. The decision rule g is defined as follows: $g = \Pi''(\frac{L}{C_t})$.

4.2.2.2 Mechanism design and derivation of the decision rule

The proposed mechanism looks as follows:

1. The firm reports its costs, i.e. the share of labor costs in the total costs $\frac{L}{C_t}$. It is possible that the firm misreports while trying to evade taxes $\frac{L}{C_t} \neq \frac{L}{C_t}'$.

2. The government decides about the decision rule g. It determines the tax rule on the basis of which tax is calculated, $\Pi'', g = \Pi''(\frac{L}{C_t})$.

3. Taxes and capital income are calculated. The firm pays taxes T to the budget and gets income on the invested capital I.

Below we will show the government's decision rule (mechanism)[19].

The market value of the sold goods equals

$V = K + \pi$, where K total costs and π profit (economic surplus).

The total costs are divided into labor costs L, costs of goods sold C and capital income I. The capital income is identified with its rate of return, the so called price of capital determined by supply and demand on it. The demand for capital depends in our model on the demand for goods.

In the literature on taxation of capital income[20] it is standard to distinguish depreciation in the replacement cost sense and economic value of an asset. If these two values coincide, the asset owner earns no pure profits. If they do not coincide the owner earns pure profits (or economic rents). Economic rents are considered as those earned in excess of the replacement cost value of asset[21].

[19] The mechanism is quite universal. On general description see Zolotarevich, K., 2002.

[20] See, for example, Bond and Devereux, 1995.

[21] Bond and Devereux proposed the neutral business tax which is levied on economic rents, for further details see Bond, S., Devereux, M., 1995, p.5.

The pure profits (economic surplus) consist of the part going to the budget in form of taxes T and the part which forms the after-tax profit of the firm Π. Analogously with capital income which, according to Marshall, can be defined as quasi-rent, the taxes can be interpreted as the income of society. We assume there is no VAT and employees' incomes are taxed separately. Taxes in our model are only one single general tax paid by the firm under decision rule[22].

Consequently, T is added to the costs, and the market value of the sold goods looks as follows

$$V = I + C + L + T + \Pi,$$

where I capital income, C other costs, L labor costs, T taxes and Π pure profit of the firm.

We employ the classical approach and try to identify the social rate of profit, on the basis of which taxes and capital income can be calculated.

In the classical theory the rate of economic surplus (economic surplus is a sum of taxes and pure profits $\pi = T + \Pi$) is defined as

$$\pi' = \frac{\pi}{L},$$

consequently

$$\pi = \pi' * L. \tag{4.51}$$

The rate of after-tax profit is

$$\Pi' = \frac{\pi}{C_t}, \tag{4.52}$$

where $C_t = C + L$.

Substituting (4.51) in (4.52) we get the rate of after-tax profit as

$$\Pi' = \pi' * \frac{L}{C_t}. \tag{4.53}$$

If $L = C_t$ then $\Pi' = \pi'$

Normally $L \leq C_t$ or $\frac{L}{C_t} \leq 1 \Rightarrow \Pi' \leq \pi'$

Moreover, with $L \to 0$

[22]We can call it corporate or firm's tax as if the whole corporate tax burden is captured by this single tax. The firm usually does not differentiate between different taxes being more interested in the whole tax burden levied on profits.

$$\lim_{L\to 0} \pi' * \frac{L}{C_t} \to 0, \tag{4.54}$$

whereas

$$\lim_{L\to 0} \frac{\pi}{L} \to \infty \tag{4.55}$$

With decrease of labor costs the rate of after-tax profit will diminish (4.54) whereas the rate of economic surplus will increase (4.55). This increase can also be due to technological progress that becomes apparent through savings in labor costs.

With the increase of the rate of economic surplus the rate of after-tax profit will decrease and limit to zero. In order to impede the decrease of the after-tax profit rate on the invested capital ($C = C_t - L$) the increase of the economic surplus should be retarded. This "braking" can be achieved through taking a quadratic root. In the following we will consider the social rate of economic surplus as a quadratic root of the actual rate of surplus in order to make it possible to impede the decrease of the after-tax profit rate

$$\pi'' = \sqrt{\pi'} = \sqrt{\Pi' * \frac{C_t}{L}}. \tag{4.56}$$

Employing equation 4.53 to derive the social rate of after-tax profit we get

$$\Pi'' = \sqrt{\Pi' * \frac{C_t}{L}} * \frac{L}{C_t}. \tag{4.57}$$

We can use the rate of after-tax profit Π' to calculate the social rate of after-tax profit Π''. Π'' as a decision rule set up by the government can be interpreted as a tax rate. Consequently, it can be employed to define the taxes T (a part of economic rent) and capital income (profit of capital owners, capital income or quasi-rent). We define taxes and capital income as follows

$$T = \Pi'' * C_t = \sqrt{\Pi' * \frac{C_t}{L}} * \frac{L}{C_t} * C_t = \pi'' * L \tag{4.58}$$

$$I = \Pi'' * C \tag{4.59}$$

We need to prove that the proposed mechanism makes it unprofitable for the firm to distort the values of costs and profits. Under the new mechanism misreporting $\frac{L}{C_t}$ allows the firm to realize lower level of profits I. Thus the firm is able to get higher capital income when reporting truthful values. See the numerical example (Table 4.1). Note that the firm cares about the maximization of its capital income I so that it will not be optimal to report, for example, 4,36 in taxes (column 8 of the table 4.1) as the level of capital income will be minimum in this case (4,31 from the table 4.1).

The firm will care about the maximization of I, max $u(I, \theta)$. Under- and over-reporting of the share of labor costs in the total costs will make the firm worse off in this case.

Suppose the firm underreports. That is what actually happens when tax evasion takes place. The substitution of labor costs for other costs and also the overstatement of other costs let the share of labor costs in total costs $\frac{L}{C_t}$ approach zero. Consequently,

$$\lim_{\frac{L}{C_t} \to 0} \Pi'' \to 0.$$

The social rate of profit approaches its lowest level, and the firm earns the lowest level of capital income.

Actually over-reporting does not happen by tax evasion, but maybe the firm will try to reach the highest possible social rate of profit. With over-reporting the share of labor costs in the total costs will limit to 1, consequently Π'' will take higher values. But as the firm substitutes C for L in this case it can not reach the maximum values of capital income I on the invested capital C (see the value of I in the first column 12,47 which is less than its maximum 18,99 in the third column).

The numerical example assumes that the firm under-reports its labor costs L and over-reports other costs C as it is normally the case by tax evasion. Consequently, the share of labor costs in total costs is diminished from 67 to 1 percent. Results for the social rate of profit Π'' and the corresponding values of taxes T and capital income I are shown in Table 4.1. The firm is worse off if it underreports L and overreports C. The firm will get the highest level of profits in terms of capital income with $\frac{L}{C_t} = 0,3$. In this example the firm also earns pure profits in the short run. In the long run pure profits are likely to disappear.

In this model we assume that there is no VAT. With VAT firms will still have incentives to increase their costs C using, for example, fake contracts with fly-by-night companies.

The mechanism has the following advantages:

1. The manipulation with expenses and profits in order to evade taxes is made unprofitable.

Table 4.1: Numerical Example

V (revenues)	100	100	100	100	100	100	100	100
L (labor costs)	20	15	13	10	8	5	3	1
C (costs of goods sold)	10	20	30	40	50	60	70	80
L+C	30	35	43	50	58	65	73	81
L/(L+C)	0,67	0,43	0,30	0,20	0,14	0,08	0,04	0,01
π (profit or economic surplus)	70	65	57	50	42	35	27	19
π' (rate of economic surplus)	3,50	4,33	4,38	5,00	5,25	7,00	9,00	19,00
Π' (rate of after-tax profit)	2,33	1,86	1,33	1,00	0,72	0,54	0,37	0,23
π'' (social rate of economic surplus)	1,87	2,08	2,09	2,24	2,29	2,65	3,00	4,36
Π'' (social rate of after-tax profit)	1,25	0,89	0,63	0,45	0,32	0,20	0,12	0,05
I (capital income)	12,47	17,84	18,99	17,89	15,80	12,21	8,63	4,31
T (taxes)	37,42	31,22	27,22	22,36	18,33	13,23	9,00	4,36
Π (pure profits)	20,11	15,93	10,79	9,75	7,87	9,56	9,37	10,34
V=L+C+I+T+Π	100	100	100	100	100	100	100	100

Source: Author's own calculations

2. The possibility of corruption and extortion by the government is minimized since firms can calculate taxes on their own depending on the proportion of labor costs in total costs.

3. It only determines the one tax rate as social rate of after-tax profit instead of many taxes and constant changes of tax rates and bases.

The mechanism will be particularly relevant for the natural resource sector due to the following reasons.

1. The problem of the natural resource companies' profit tax evasion can be alleviated. Now the government tries to expropriate in form of taxes (mostly indirect taxes) up to 100 percent of pure profits generated in the industry[23]. The firms try to evade profit tax in order to secure some part of pure profits using the offshore companies as intermediaries. They claim that otherwise they are not rewarded for working in the industry and are compelled to evade to be able to make some investments.

2. Firms can be stimulated to invest their own capital in the industry. First of all it concerns fields and deposits which are extremely difficult to explore. At the moment, firms are reluctant to invest unless the government grants them favorable tax conditions. Unfortunately, standard tax advantages are normally misused by companies and state officials, and open up opportunities for corruption.

3. Capital income will grow with wages.

4.3 Summary

The purpose of this chapter was to explore corporate tax evasion caused mainly by governments. Since Russia serves as a good example for bad government practices (since corruption is very high and recently many cases of extortion have been reported) tax evasion can be partly explained by government behavior.

In the *first model* we assumed that there are two types of government: the good one which is interested in detecting and penalizing tax evasion, and the bad one which extorts monies from firms. In the static game we additionally assumed that the government also knows the relative level of firms' profits in terms that it is able to distinguish between small and big firms in their profit generation ability.

[23]For details see Chernyshov, S., 2005, Taxes - a Russian paradox, http://www.bdo.ru/eng/press/marketnews/?form=print??id=1903.

We have shown that the firm's equilibrium belief about the type it faces depends solely on the penalties on detected tax evasion applied by the good government and not on the extortion parameter of the bad type of government. If the probability of bad government is high and standard penalties for tax evasion are applied the firm's optimal reaction will be to evade. The payoff from evasion will be higher than from non-evasion. Consequently, the deterrent effect of penalties may be alleviated, and the higher probability of facing a bad government the higher the level of tax evasion is observed. Frequent audits of good government may not deter a firm from evasion. A pure evasion equilibrium is observed with the higher probability of bad government.

The firm which evades taxes can bribe the government in order to escape extortion. The bribe decreases the equilibrium belief about the government type. It pays to evade taxes even with a lower probability of facing the bad government. Consequently, bribery intensifies tax evasion even more.

As the tax rate rises, evasion pays more in the pure evasion equilibrium. But the evasion decision is not influenced by tax rate increase in the hybrid equilibrium (if the penalty is proportional to evaded taxes). Tax evasion may increase even for a small probability of bad government due to rise of tax rate.

In the *dynamic game*, the government observes firm's profits which are now firm's private information and chooses whether to audit, to extort or to do nothing. A firm in its turn decides in its profit declaration for tax purposes while being uncertain about the objective of the government. Again two government types are assumed: good and bad.

The main results are the following. With a higher probability of facing a bad government, the good government needs to exert higher auditing efforts to prevent tax evasion. Moreover, in the so called audit-evasion equilibrium the firm will evade taxes even being audited with certainty by the good government if there is a high probability of facing a bad government. If extortion takes place it will pay to evade taxes because the payoff will be higher under evasion. Consequently, the potential for extortion undermines revenue collection of good government. The result also holds even if extortion is costly. Extortion is also possible in the mixed evasion equilibrium where the firm and the good government are indifferent to their actions (evade or not, audit or do nothing).

In the presence of bad government the deterrent effect of penalties and audits is alleviated. Being increased they may not produce the desired reduction in the evasion level. The firm can still evade if the probability of bad government is high enough. Even higher penalties will be needed to deter firms from evasion.

More incentives to evade provided by the presence of the bad government induce the good government to audit more to prevent evasion. This produces audit costs which will be higher the higher the probability of facing a bad government is. Consequently, resources may be lost.

The main points which we highlighted from these models are the following: 1) The prior probability of facing an extortionist government increases tax evasion incentives.

2) Audits and penalties applied by good government may not be effective in combatting tax evasion due to bad government.

We conclude that some part of tax evasion can be explained by the existence of bad governments. The other part is associated with techniques which firms practice in order to reduce the level of tax bases.

In the *next model* we analyzed tax evasion techniques of firms. They are basically reduced to the manipulation of labor costs and profits. As the government may influence tax rates and concealment costs to some extent to reduce profit from evasion, it is still difficult to monitor actual costs and profits.

We were interested in effects of tax policy parameters in order to decrease company profit from evasion and to deter firms from expenses and profits manipulation. The decrease of profit and payroll tax rates contributes to the reduction of profit from evasion. Higher concealment costs have also negative effect on profit from evasion. But as the level of profits and labor costs are parameters which are chosen by firm, the incentive to distort them in order to gain some additional profit from tax evasion is still present.

The mechanism which can potentially alleviate the firms' incentive to misreport costs and profits is proposed. It is based on the calculation of tax and profits on the basis of the social rate of after-tax profit. We propose a single tax rate to be levied on companies. Analogously to tax rates set up by the state, the social rate of after-tax profit is a decision rule to determine this tax rate. This mechanism is particularly useful for companies in the natural resource sector where high evasion of profit tax is observed.

Chapter 5

Policy implications

In the last years Russia seems to have worried less about the problem of tax evasion since losses in budget revenues are not acute nowadays due to the high oil prices on world markets[1]. Moreover, the stabilization fund created to accumulate excess oil dollars is supposed to solve the budget deficit in the future if prices are not so favorable.

Apart from tax reform and the demonstrative trial against one big oil enterprise which served indirectly to combat tax evasion, only a few measures have been taken to minimize the tax gap and increase tax compliance. At the same time, the level of tax compliance among firms remains low. There are still certain problems within tax administration.

Tax reform did much in terms of efficiency of the tax system. In some aspects parallels can be drawn with "tax reform of the eighties" - the world-wide tax reform movement with common characteristics of reductions in personal and corporate income tax rates allied to base broadening and a change in tax mix towards an increase in indirect taxation[2].

The Russian tax system was also simplified, with the number of taxes reduced, which could partially curtail the "grabbing hand of the state" especially on local and regional levels. It was the only measure apart from the elimination of tax concessions which was implemented to minimize evasion opportunities. Reduction of tax rates has indirectly reduced the net advantages of tax evasion to some extent.

It is worth to notify that "tax reform of the eighties" was also intended to combat evasion and avoidance practices, widespread at that time. But the undertaken measures were mainly of administrative character such as deduction at source, tightening up on tax administration and self-assessment[3].

---

[1]On July 2006 it reached new highs, pushing above 75 USD a barrel.

[2]For details see Sandford, C., p.156-196.

[3]ibid., p.160

Russia is supposed to face more challenging tasks in order to reduce evasion opportunities, which are buried in the functioning of tax administration and other state institutions, and to promote voluntary tax compliance. As far as the economic approach is concerned, Russia has done much in terms of tax rate reduction. On the other hand, Russia should reconsider or even restrain its penalization and audit policies at least until the time when evasion opportunities connected with the functioning of state institutions is minimized.

We begin this chapter by considering policy implications for the tax system. Instruments of tax policy are used extensively to combat tax evasion, but are very controversial in the theoretical and empirical context. Then we discuss institutional aspects, focusing on corruption and extortion which explain a large part of tax evasion in Russia, but at the same time no active policy measures have been taken in this respect. As a result, corruption has even increased in the last years. In the end we analyze some social and behavioral aspects aimed at increasing the overall voluntary tax compliance in the society.

Combatting tax evasion is not an easy task especially when tax evasion in the country is aggravated by corruption and the overall unwillingness to pay taxes. Reducing net advantages for tax evasion through changes in penalties, tax rates, probabilities of audits, can be implemented in the short run, whereas combatting corruption can be considered as a more challenging task with no speedy results. Even more time is also needed for improvement of the social norms in society.

These three blocks - tax policy issues, institutional aspects and promotion of voluntary compliance - relevant for reducing tax evasion can be also considered as subsequent policy steps. The state decides on tax policy issues which are more appropriate in the present country-specific environment, then takes on measures to tackle corruption. And only after the state reconsiders the way it carries out its functions can the willingness to evade taxes be reduced among taxpayers.

5.1 Tax policy

Governments resort to the instruments of the tax system in order to reduce evasion. These are penalties, tax rates and probabilities of investigation - the tools employed from the basic theoretical analysis of crime extended to the case of tax evasion. Tax regimes are often seen as simplified tax practices, where the calculation of taxes is based on a firm's observable characteristics through which the understating or hiding of tax bases is minimized.

We start with penalties and audits since our main results concern these measures of tax policy. Then we discuss tax rates and tax regimes.

5.1.1 Penalties

Normally increasing penalties is a good measure to decrease tax evasion. Moreover, the penalties are advised to be set very high since they are not connected with any costs to the state, but their deterrent effect is significant.

Two aspects are to be considered in this connection which question the policy prescription to increase penalties.

1. Non-benevolent governments can alleviate the penalties' deterrent effect.

We have shown that if there is a bad government which penalizes arbitrarily, for example in form of extortion the firm's belief about the government type which makes it indifferent between evasion and non evasion depends solely on the penalties for tax evasion applied by the good government. If the probability of facing bad government is high for the firm, and the penalties applied by the good government are standard (normally they are 15-20 percent of the taxes unpaid) it may cause the switch to the pure evasion equilibrium. Higher evasion levels are observed in the economy with the bad government.

Consequently, when penalties for tax evasion are increased by the good government the desired effect of tax evasion reduction may not be observed if the probability of facing a crooked government is too high. So that this increase may not be high enough to deter a firm from tax evasion.

Very high penalties may be counter-productive since severe penalization of some tax evaders may be perceived harsh by society, developing an anti-government (tax authorities) attitudes. Even honest firms will be threatened. They can thus incur higher compliance costs becoming over-meticulous with their tax-record keeping[4]. If corruption or extortion of state officials is observed, taxpayers may find it optimal to switch to tax evasion, for example, if compliance costs will be higher than the level of bribes or extortion money.

The basic theory of Allingham and Sandmo implies that the optimal policy to combat tax evasion is to make the penalties very high and costs of administration very low[5]. What actually is going on when the collection costs are minimized is the fact that tax officials try to collect taxes which are

[4] Sandford, C., p.151.

[5] As Kolm put it "hang tax evaders with probability zero", see Kolm, S.-K. (1973).

easier to collect, and to target only large taxpayers, normally big companies[6]. The first case leads to the collection of indirect taxes such as VAT, excise, customs duties and to problem of collecting profit taxes. The problem of profit tax collection from oil companies was recently reported as one of the most serious form of tax evasion in Russia.

It also worth to notify that chasing only big companies is an indirect indication that evasion is condoned by society[7]. Collection costs are thus traded off for compliance and welfare costs. Higher compliance costs also induce firms to keep tax departments which are constantly looking for loopholes in the tax law and practice massive avoidance.

Minimization of collection costs may also invite corruption. In reality it is extremely difficult to prove after some time that corruption took place between a firm and a tax official. Normally such cases are opened at the moment when handing over of the bribe happens. It is extremely difficult to open up corruption cases thereafter. As the evidence also shows, giving bribes doesn't mean any guarantees to the firm that it won't be penalized for tax evasion in the future.

Higher penalties can be also counterproductive in a sense that they can induce more investigations from the tax organs each of which can potentially end up in bribery. Consequently, tax evasion because of corruption can even increase. Furthermore, higher penalties are normally associated with higher bribes required to hide tax evasion. Thus corruption can be exacerbated instead of evasion being reduced. Although the normal reaction of the firm to increased fines is to reduce its evasion level, in case of non-benevolent governments this effect can be distorted.

Consequently, the optimal policy of very high penalties and small audit probabilities has its limitations so that its practical implementation may be arguable.

The effect of higher penalties on tax evasion may be positive if public officials are corrupt or a high level of corruption is a observed in the economy[8]. Thus it can be proposed that the state should deter from any increase in penalties for tax evasion as an instrument to reduce tax evasion unless the corruption level is reduced and extortion is combatted.

---

[6]See, Tanzi, V., p.177.

[7]In Russia a lot of small companies don't pay their taxes at all operating completely underground.

[8]Cule, M. and Fulton, M. (2005) proved that increase in the penalty rate or firm auditing leads to more tax evasion due to the complementarity that exists between cheating and corruption, p.210.

2. The second aspect to be outlined is that firms are not the same as individual taxpayers.

Although owned and managed by individual taxpayers, firms are more driven by economic incentives. Their perceptions and beliefs are more based on observable policy parameters including penalties, than for example behavioral aspects.

As individuals may be risk-averse or driven by intrinsic honesty, firms are more responsive to instruments of tax policy. We have shown that firm belief about the government type depends in case of bad government extortion only on penalties on tax evaders applied by good government. Consequently, increased penalties may actually reinforce the firm's belief that the probability of bad government is quite high.

It is also important who is actually penalized within the firm. In this respect the separation of ownership and control is the distinguished feature of corporate tax evasion analysis which says that heavier penalties on managers will help to reduce tax evasion. As sometimes especially in Russia these relations are blurred or even the question of property rights is not clear, it may be difficult to implement this prescription in practice. Moreover, Russian firms have consolidated structures making it difficult to trace the evasion chain.

As firms pay different taxes, and are also tax agents, they can practice different evasion activities, some of which can be more successful, others may be more risky. They also incur more compliance costs since they are doing significant work calculating and collecting taxes for the government. Since penalties are normally the same for all taxes, their increase may lead to more evasion of those taxes which are easier to dodge, or, in case of corruption, which may be easier colluded with the state officials. The situation can be observed in Russia where profit taxes are among the most evaded, whereas indirect taxes, especially resource payments, are collected better now[9].

If the state would like to use severe penalties as deterrent for evasion, their transparency and equitable application should be guaranteed. After observing the severe penalization of some tax evaders other firms can be threatened. If transparency is not provided through the law, and firms can not count on the promises of the state, it may be dangerous since the normal response to reduce tax evasion is likely to be distorted.

Relating the above to the basic theory of tax evasion, it can be concluded that in case of facing non-benevolent government the risk-neutral firm simply does not know whether it will be penalized for tax evasion or not (or it is also

[9] See Vasiljeva, A., Gurvich, E., Subbotin, V., 2003, p.13.

possible to be penalized for non-evasion), which penalties would be applied in case of penalization, and whether there are opportunities to escape them. Taking into account these factors it may be difficult to conclude about the deterrent effect of penalties on tax evasion, since due to them the firm's evasion decision may be distorted.

Based on the country-specific theoretical conclusions and the observed evidence we propose that the state should not use penalties as an instrument to deter evasion unless at least other more long-term problems are solved. These problems are connected to the appropriate functioning of state institutions.

5.1.2 Audits

Frequent audits are the second element of tax policy which are usually used to reduce evasion. As penalties can be applied to chosen taxpayers, strict auditing is more equitable if applied to many tax evaders. Being correctly implemented they can deter firms from evasion. But

1. The deterrent effect of audits may be minimized if extortion among state officials takes place. The higher the probability of facing a bad government which extorts monies from firms, the higher the probability of an audit of the good government has to be to prevent evasion. There is an equilibrium where the profitable firm will always evade taxes even if it is audited with certainty by the good government. The driving force behind this equilibrium is a high probability of facing a crook government. Then it pays to evade because the payoff will be higher under evasion if extortion takes place.

Consequently, the deterrent effect of audits can even be neglected. The "quality" of government plays a crucial role in application of audits.

2. Audits are costly for the state. It is considered as one of the most important reasons for not using audits extensively. We have also shown that the presence of bad governments increases the expected audit costs and thus produces more welfare losses. The expected audit cost will increase with the probability of facing a bad government.

The efficiency question arises: the additional resources should be employed in tax administration up to the point where marginal costs will not exceed the marginal tax revenues collected from tax evaders as a result of auditing. This question is very difficult to answer due to the practical problems of counting and measuring costs and revenues as well as some fundamental problems of audit applications[10]. For example, on one hand, considered as

[10]See Sandford, C., p. 144-145.

crime, tax evasion should be combatted with all available resources. On the other hand, it is not perceived as a usual crime and thus audits primarily aim to threaten taxpayers.

The practice shows that more successful results were achieved when the investigation efforts were not spontaneous but were implemented through particular programmes. Only in this case can it be guaranteed that the revenues put into tax administration will not be lost[11].

3. Audits can be perceived as negative by firms, compelling them to incur more compliance costs in order to hide tax evasion or to check out their tax record-keeping. As with penalties, giving bribes may be less costly for firms if the government is corrupt. So even the previously honest taxpayers may switch to tax evasion. Consequently, in case of audits, not only collection costs will be higher, but compliance costs to taxpayers can also increase.

We have shown that in case of corruption increasing penalties for tax evasion may lead to more investigations from tax officials. As it can be observed from the Russian reality these investigations were not connected with receiving additional resources from the state for this purpose. This "voluntary commitment" can be considered as an opportunity to extort additional bribes from the firms, and thus can not lead to the decreased evasion. Audits in this sense become counterproductive and their application may not result in less evasion.

If the government audits firms in an unsystematic, discretionary manner, the firms will not be able to quantify the probability of detection correctly considering detection as an unsystematic risk. Therefore the effect of audits on tax evasion will be significantly reduced.

It is also argued that in Russia, due to the discretionary power of authorities inherited from the socialist area and still observed, the enforcement policy can bring opposite results or may be ineffective in combatting tax evasion.

If applied, the enforcement policy should be more transparent and equitable. Thus in a country where evasion is epidemic investigations should cover all companies, but the area of investigation should be limited. The concentration can be on particular taxes or a particular tax period, for example, only one year or only current tax obligations. It can thus discipline firms which will be compelled to improve their book-keeping, but not to increase their compliance costs when records for many previous years are investigated. Investigations applied to all firms may potentially diminish the discretionary behavior and corruption of tax officials through increased transparency of the process.

[11]See Sandford, C., p. 144-145.

Audits are connected with investigation costs incurred by the state. It can be proposed that the resources which are put into tax administration should go into the development of tax administration itself. They should also apply some selected methods aimed for instance at better targeting of tax evaders or areas where the tax revenue loss is huge.

5.1.3 Tax rates

Normally, reduction of tax rates is seen to be a good policy instrument to combat tax evasion. Moreover, this argument is stronger in case of corporate evasion since no ambiguity of the effect of tax rate is observed in the models.

But as the penalties are usually a fixed percentage of unpaid taxes, the reduction of tax rates is connected with the reduction of penalties which may offset the effect of decreased evasion.

The stronger support to the lower tax rates in reducing evasion is also associated with the fact that firms are normally assumed to be neutral. Consequently, for example, the argument that the taxpayer's risk-aversion which increases with income may affect tax evasion due to the reduction of the tax rate in the opposite way does not appear in corporate tax evasion.

The empirical support that low tax rates are associated with less tax evasion is not found in developed countries where firms being burdened with higher tax rates evade less than firms in transition and developing economies where tax rates are normally lower. Thus the argument that tax rates' reduction may immediately help to reduce evasion in a country is arguable. Other aspects such as state institutions play more important role.

In Russia the tax rates are not set high in comparison with developed and some transition economies, but rather high implicit tax rates associated with additional compliance and concealment costs can be observed. So we propose that further decrease of tax rates will not bring any significant effect on the reduction of tax evasion[12] whereas an increase of tax rates may cause the tax evasion to rise.

Consequently, the state should carefully consider any step connected with tax rate reduction since a later rise may have a negative effect initiating a new jump in the level of tax evasion. Reduction of the tax rates must be also carefully assessed for the long term perspective. For example, in case of effectual budget revenues when oil prices are high the state should not immediately lower tax rates which it will be forced to rise again under another economic situation, but concentrate on efforts to increase the overall tax compliance.

[12] Firms' tax evasion hasn't significantly decreased after the tax reform.

On the whole, increase of tax rates causes tax evasion to rise, whereas there is little evidence that a decrease of rates itself produces a significant increase in overall tax compliance.

5.1.4 Tax regimes

Tax regimes should aim to address the specific problems in corporate evading activities thus minimizing opportunities for them. For example, taxation on withholding basis helps to reduce income tax evasion of individual taxpayers promoting deduction at source. Among firms the opportunities for tax evasion can be reduced mainly by a simplified tax structure, and this feature is more often addressed in designing the special tax regimes.

A simple and equitable tax system is often advised as more appropriate in the presence of tax evasion[13]. Consequently, tax advantages are not welcomed. As they open opportunities for evasion due to the ambiguity of the tax law as well as for corruption they are advised to be abolished. In Russia it was implemented as a part of profit tax reform. Since an overstating of tax exemptions, allowances, reliefs, credits is one of the main form of corporate evasion it seems to be a good policy measure. Although, on the other side, with the intention to stimulate investments, there are attempts to restore investment credits as well as to provide tax advantages for oil companies which explore natural resources under unfavorable conditions. But there are still fears that these tax concessions can be misused to hide taxes.

Apart from tax advantages some tax regimes are seen as instruments to rise tax compliance and create a favorable tax environment for some companies especially for small and medium-sized business, also with the aim to bring them out of the shadow economy and eventually later to the "normal" tax system. Simplified and presumptive tax regimes are applied in Russia. The first regime considers payment of one tax instead of several taxes, the other tries to estimate income of a company on the basis of sales statistics and other criteria (employees, floor space and so on). Although it is propagated that such systems support small business development, their primary aim is to collect some tax revenues from them. No wonder these systems are extensively used in developing countries. For example, Argentina and Mexico introduced a system of minimum income tax for companies and individuals which is based on gross assets[14].

In Russia the functioning of these regimes seems attractive for many firms: they try to be taxed under the simplified regime thus escaping the

---

[13]See, for example, Thiessen, U., 2003.

[14]See, Tanzi, V., 2000, A primer on tax evasion, in: Policies, Institutions and the Dark Side of Economics, Chentelham, Elgar, p.179.

regular system and discretionary power of the authorities. Moreover, individual taxpayers resort to the simplified system which allows to pay 6 percent of income tax instead of 13 percent according to the normal individual income tax regime. It is also argued that such regimes can not be considered in the long-run since the tax base should be determined as a result of economic activity.

In order to reduce tax evasion two main aspects should be taken into account when proposing a special tax regime:

1. For tax officials the calculation of taxes should be based on observable data which firms have no incentive to distort.

2. For firms the discretion of state officials should be minimized so that in the best case they can calculate their taxes without incurring much compliance costs. Self-assessment will be in this case the best solution for companies.

In this regard we have proposed a tax regime which allows to calculate taxes and profits on the basis of the share of labor costs in total costs. Analogously with the tax rate the state sets up the rule of the tax rate's determination. The mechanism can be especially useful in taxation of natural resource companies. At the moment there is a critical situation with profit tax evasion. Having difficulties to evade VAT, export duty and tax on oil extraction which are imposed ad valorem based on world oil price, the evasion of profit tax is left as the only opportunity to hide a part of pure profits. Moreover, the state reconsiders regularly the amount of indirect taxes which cause uproar among oil companies as they claim almost 100 percent of their pure profits go to the budget. Consequently, they have no money and incentives to invest in the natural resource industry.

The situation can be potentially dangerous for the Russian economy on the whole. Natural resource industry is practically the only competitive advantage of the country. Moreover, most reserves require large investments to be explored. Other countries such as Saudi Arabia invest a lot in production and oil refinery, Singapore earns its main income from oil refinery. Russia delivers on the world markets oil of a poor quality. Consequently, it is also important to stimulate Russian firms to invest. With potential risk of nationalization, firms are more reluctant to do it preferring to transfer profits abroad using offshores and transfer pricing thus evading profit taxes. What they actually do by this kind of evasion is the following: they establish an intermediate firm offshore and sell oil to this offshore company which accumulates profits. In spite of the fact that officially the tax burden on the oil and gas sector is high, it is not so in reality when profits are evaded through intermediaries.

Some steps have already been done to create a special regime of taxation for natural resource companies. Thus tax on natural resource's extraction was introduced, and its tax base is now modified according not to domestic oil prices as it was before, but to the world prices. This does not allow oil companies to reduce the tax base with the help of transfer pricing inside Russia. Ideally the differentiation of this tax could potentially solve the problem of exploration under different natural and economic conditions. But implementation of this kind of differentiation in reality can lead to arbitrariness of the state officials when they may determine lower tax rates pursuing their own interest[15].

To alleviate these and some other problems we have described a mechanism which can be potentially used as a model of a tax regime for the natural resource sector. As it was proposed the state analogously with setting of a tax rate establishes a rule of calculating the social rate of after-tax profit which is divided between the state in form of taxes and a firm in form of capital income. The remaining pure profits earned due to the favorable economic situation can be accumulated in the stabilization fund which is now formed of additional income earned from oil sales.

We have shown that the incentives to overstate labor costs and to understate other costs thus distorting profits and evading due taxes are not observed. Arbitrariness and corruption of the state officials is alleviated since there is little scope left for manipulation with the observable data. Self-assessment will be introduced which allows companies to reduce potential contacts with tax administration.

In a situation of favorable oil prices the state tries to tax heavily the oil sector extracting almost 100 percent of its pure profits using indirect taxation leaving no incentives to invest in a highly profitable industry. With the proposed mechanism firms will be rewarded according to their investments.

5.2 Institutional aspects

The institutional aspects are staying apart from the scope of the tax system, but as it was shown they cause and influence the problem of tax evasion. Consequently, combatting tax evasion without tackling these issues can be unproductive. We propose that two problems deserve the primary concern. Combatting corruption and extortion can be seen as a main problem in functioning of state institutions, since a large part of tax evasion is connected

[15]Companies also escape the tax on natural resources' extraction by hiding the extracted oil which are not entitled for export.

with bribery. Improvement of social norms encompasses all previously discussed aspects. Relationships between state and society are considered on the whole, as well as complexities of this cooperation between the state and companies in particular.

5.2.1 Combatting corruption and extortion

While speaking about tax evasion it is normally assumed that taxpayers cheat the government and appropriate a part or all of tax revenues assigned to the state. In fact it is only a part of tax evasion which appears due to tax evading activities of taxpayers. The other part of tax evasion can be explained by corruption so that the whole evasion is bigger if there is corruption in the country. Corrupt tax practices involve collusion between taxpayers and government officials.

From a different perspective, corruption creates an additional tax burden. It actually acts like an arbitrary applied additional tax. In international comparison, Russia has low tax rates, but at the same time taxpayers say that the tax burden is very high. Assuming that the tax burden is comprised of the tax rates and the operation of the tax system one can conclude that the problem of the additional tax burden lies not in the tax system itself, but in its functioning. The state does not carry out its functions in the process of tax collection properly. The government role as well as the tax system are thus distorted.

Recent investigations[16] provided new evidence that corruption effects the structure of taxes: it can explain the predominance of indirect taxes in total tax revenues in the presence of higher corruption in developing countries. Although there is no such survey for transition economies it can also explain the prevalence of indirect taxes as a main source of budget revenues such as, for example, export duties collected from oil companies in Russia[17].

Higher corruption is associated with lower revenues of all types, except for revenues from natural resources. The abundance of natural resources is also shown to be an important determinant of corruption[18].

As we consider corruption specifically in connection with tax evasion, the measures to combat the former which will potentially reduce the latter should be divided into direct and indirect measures. The first are common tools to

[16] See Tanzi, V. and Davoodi, H., 2000.

[17] Indirect taxes including the revenues from external economic activity and use of natural resources comprise 78.4 percent of GDP in 2005. For comparison income, profit and social taxes account for 15.8, see The Federal Bill "On the Federal Budget for 2005".

[18] See Tanzi, V. and Davoodi, H.R., 2000, p.18.

reduce corruption on the whole, the second are connected with the particular steps of tax reforms.

Many authors[19] argue that to bring demand and supply for bribery down the way the state carries out its functions should be changed. Moreover, it means the assessments of country-specific incentives which encourage corruption. It is often argued that the wages of public officials should be increased or just set very high to deter them from taking bribes. As an example, Singapur is often sited where the wage level of the state officials is the highest in the world. In Russia, on the contrary, public jobs are low-paid, but especially demanded at tax departments and police where there are plenty of opportunities for bribery.

Increased salaries do not mean that state officials automatically refuse bribes. Due to the low payment and deteriorated image of public jobs they do not attract better qualified and responsible people. On the other hand, traditionally state employees are given more rights and benefits from the state itself so that many people consider the state job as an opportunity to receive more non-monetary benefits and power according to the positions held. On all levels good connections and relationships are needed to get any kind of the state job. Consequently, we can not conclude that with higher salaries public officials refuse bribes or that better people will be necessarily attracted.

As with penalties for tax evasion harsh penalties for corruption are supposed to reduce its level. But as Mookherjee and Png (1995) argue, raising penalties for corruption may cause an increase of primary harm (in our case tax evasion, although they considered pollution). This result is due to the fact that authorities will investigate less if they are penalized for corruption. Reduced audits cause firms to evade more. But on the other side, investigations in a corruptive environment do not necessarily reduce evasion since it may cause more bribes.

Penalties for corruption are quite specific: they are usually very harsh in Russia, so that losing a job is a minimum penalty which can be applied. But corruption is normally very difficult to detect. The efficient system of penalization should thus concentrate more on the later aspect. Penalties should rather play a secondary role. Due to the secrecy of the transaction and the lack of proven evidence thereafter the process of penalization is complicated.

The country-specific evidence also suggests that in Russia the arbitrary penalization for tax evasion from the government is likely to be endogenized. Politicians adjust the level of interventions in the private sector. They can

[19] For example, Tanzi, V., Kaufmann, D..

be favorable to some taxpayers whereas they can apply harsh penalties for evasion to others. It can also mean that they may accept bribes from all enterprises but keep secrecy only in certain cases.

Two policy conclusions can be made:
1. Penalties for corruption do not play an important role. On the one hand, they may be productive if detection of corruption is efficient, but on the other hand, they may also deter tax officials from any investigation, especially when they are underpaid. Higher salaries can not be seen as a solution as well, but rather the employment system must be changed.
2. As such practices are more visible on the higher levels and concern big companies, political leaders should commit to honest behavior.

Some cultural peculiarities of the penalization practice inherited from the Soviet era can influence the application of penalties if the state takes on harsh enforcement and total control. In sum, the Russian specific requires to concentrate rather on incentives which will discourage corruption from both sides as well on systematic reforms. Among these indirect instruments which could also reduce tax evasion induced by corruption the following are recommended:

1. Simplified tax rules as well as abolition of regulations regarding taxes should be promoted.
2. Companies should assess due taxes on their own so that the work of a tax inspector would be reduced to distant control. Evidence indicates that enterprises normally pay unofficially for visits to tax inspectors[20] in order to be treated "nicely".

Sometimes it is proposed that taxes should be collected by an independent tax agency, which can, for example, function as a public-private partnership. In terms of increased efficiency it may be a good solution, but it can hardly solve the problem of corruption in society.

We have shown that bribery increases the firms' perception about the arbitrariness and discretion of the government (bad government). Assuming two government types - a bad one which practices extortion and a good one which is interested in investigating and penalizing tax evasion - we have shown that the higher probability of facing a bad government influences the evasion decision of the firm. Even being audited by the good government with the probability one the firm still may find it optimal to evade taxes. Moreover, auditing efforts from the good government's side must be higher

[20] See, for example, Kaufmann, D., p.176.

to deter evasion if the probability of facing a bad government is high. These efforts are thus undermined making the standard instruments to combat tax evasion less efficient.

Hindriks, Keen und Muthoo (1999) have shown that in addition to loss in tax collection, the more bribes are collected, the more a tax inspector can resort to extortion in order to collect even more.

In this concern institutional aspects are of primary importance, and Russia still needs some reforms and time in order for them to function properly. These problems are rather fundamental and do not concern the instruments of tax policy. Still such institutional characteristics as independent judicial system, free media, civil society, the existence of non-government organizations are considered to be the key features of any less corrupt society. Consequently, incremental policy measures such as, for example, setting of high penalties or strict control hardly achieve results if corruption is pervasive. It is also worth mentioning here that in spite of the police state in the Soviet system, bribery was also a societal decease at that time[21].

To bring the level of corruption down, political competition should be promoted. Unfortunately, this is not the case in today's Russia. So it can be inferred that transparency of government action is not observed.

5.2.2 Improvement of the social norms

As we have already discussed, social stigmatization leads to equilibrium where massive evasion can prevail. Social norms are proved to be important determinant in tax evasion decision. Consequently, improvement of this aspect can potentially alleviate the evasion problem in the Russian economy which is characterized by the "bad" equilibrium.

We focus on the role of the state in improvement of social norms in Russian society. The process encompasses the following measures:

1. The protection of property rights.

Once defined they should be fostered. If it is considered that they have been appropriated unfairly, the state should reconsider the privatization giving the firm an opportunity to pay out the residual price in form of taxes on a deferred basis. Otherwise it contributes to the instability of the property rights structure. Since most owners of former state property got it by underhand means, and could lose it the same way[22]. As Tanzi and Davoodi note, in transition economies, ensuring that government officials and others

[21] Sec Kneen, P., 2000.

[22] See "States within the state: Russia's institutions seem designed to ensure that nothing changes", The Economist, 19 July 2001.

do not misappropriate state assets is also a hugely challenging task because of the unclear nature of property rights and enforcement problems[23].

2. Creation of the "rule of law".

Established property rights as well as other rights should be protected by an independent legal system. The independence of the legal system is questionable in Russia. Politicians have an opportunity to influence the outcome of legal process. They participate quite often in some businesses or lobby the interests of particular firms thus earning additional income for themselves which is not considered abnormal in society. Consequently, the creation of the rule of law is averted.

3. Provision of public goods.

Firms complain that they are unwilling to pay taxes unless they see that the state makes efforts to invest in public goods from which firms can profit. For companies it is relevant that their property rights will be protected by the law, they could apply and profit from well functioning state institutions, such as tax organs, courts, police and not from particular individuals on which decisions they are dependent. Because in this case it is quite natural that they are unwilling to cooperate with the state.

4. Redistribution.

Taxes in modern society are not not paid under compulsion, they are payments for the provision of state services and goods as well as funds for financing of programmes agreed by society. For example, the state can use taxes to compensate those who are unable to earn income on their own, such as children, elderly and disabled people. If this provision deteriorates, society is more unlikely to pay to the state and begins to condone tax evasion. Consequently, more transparency in spending activities of the state should be encouraged. Taking into account massive corruption in Russia it is advised that public spending be focused on education and health, and not on military and infrastructure. Mauro (1998) has shown that corrupt countries spend less on education and health.

Normally, society plays a crucial role in improvement of the social norms, and citizens should be more responsible for preventing tax evasion. As it was already pointed out firms are more driven by economic incentives, consequently, as an entity, a firm can hardly be influenced by ethical aspects. The situation in Russia is quite paradoxical in this respect since it is impossible

[23]Tanzi, V., Davoodi, H.R., 2000

for the state to build a good rapport with society and thereby to isolate the phenomenon of tax evasion for the following reasons.

In Russia individual taxpayers practically do not pay taxes. Their taxes are withheld by employers if at all, so that all taxes are usually paid by companies. Actually individual taxpayers do not care about their tax liabilities. On the other hand, they are not satisfied with redistribution as well as with public goods provision for which taxes are normally collected. In particular, high income gaps were partly compensated by the provision of non-monetary benefits in form of free medicaments, free use of public transport, some public services. Now they are replaced by additional monetary compensation which does not cover the payments of previously provided benefits. Citizens are also dissatisfied with the quality of the medical service. The state in its turn complains that business dodges taxes. The situation when society is discontented with the state, but the state has claims on companies, can not lead to responsibility between the state and the society, and consequently, the improvement of social norms is circumvented. As long as the state does not solve the problems within state institutions the society will continue to be indifferent to the problem of tax evasion. Moreover, as these problems are solved, individual taxpayers should become responsible for paying their own taxes. Then they will be able to demand transparency from the state on what their taxes are spent on. That will help to promote civil institutions.

The realization of the first three measures - the protection of property rights, creation of the rule of law and public goods provision - are of primary importance, they should aim to build a good rapport between the state and business as a main taxpayer. It appears not to be easy since companies profit less from the state than citizens and consequently, a lower level of cooperation is presupposed. The redistributive aspect can be only adapted according to the level of this cooperation. On the whole, implementation of these measures can help to create the appropriate tax structure with efficient enforcement. It may be the structure with lower or higher tax rates although as it was already proposed in the situation of massive evasion, the tax rates should not be increased because it can provoke a shift to more evasion.

In the situation of alienation with the state due to its "bad behavior", high penalties and frequent audits are not considered to be good policy measures, especially when politicians can adjust the level of interventions. Moreover it will not signal the efficiency of the tax administration. Instead, a higher level of intelligence with appropriate rewards, and more independence from political influence should be promoted within the tax organs. If the state can realize the above-mentioned measures it will manage to lower compliance costs in society, thus increasing overall tax compliance in which case taxpayers will conform to improved social norms.

5.3 Summary

We have considered the three blocks of policy measures: tax policy instruments, which may decrease corporate tax evasion; measures to combat corruption and extortion, to improve government institutions; social norms.

As our main findings show the aspect of bad governments existence and moreover, the higher probability of facing it, increases the evasion level of firms. Application of standard instruments of tax policy, first of all, audits and penalties, appears to be limited by this aspect. Thus we get the result that even being audited with certainty by the good government, the evading firms may still find it optimal to evade taxes if extortion takes place.

The good government should also carefully consider the application of harsh penalties. We have shown that the firm's belief of facing a bad government depends in equilibrium solely on penalties applied by the good government. If this belief is high but the good government returns to the normal level of penalties, the pure evasion equilibrium is observed. The high probability of bad government which extorts, may alleviate the penalties' deterrent effect. Consequently, even if the good government increases penalties on tax evaders, the desired reduction of tax evasion may not be observed.

Careful evaluation of policy measures is needed. For example, in the case of tax rates, their increase is not advised since it may cause a leap in corporate evading activities. Consequently, the decrease should be carefully assessed.

Overall simplification of the tax system is proposed, but the drawbacks of special regimes put a question on their promotion. We have proposed an alternative tax regime, especially for the natural resource sector, to solve mainly the problem of profit tax evasion and underinvestments in this industry. Self-assessment, simplicity, as well as calculation based on observable data are key characteristics to provide a solution to these problems.

These characteristics also serve as criteria for indirect policy measures to combat corruption in the tax collection process. As for the direct measures, the following can be outlined: efficient detection of corruption and the commitment of political leaders to deter it. Public pressure seems to play a crucial role: the society should be aware of government spending policies and its abuses. Free press and non-government organizations can help to promote political competition.

Penalization for corruption will be advised to play a secondary role. Cultural aspects should also be taken into account in this concern. Russian society has already had many experiences with severe penalization for corruption, and for tax evasion as well. Still, the problems were not solved. Maybe what the society lacks is a fair treatment under the rule of law.

Creation of the "rule of law", property rights' protection, public goods's provision and efficient redistribution are seen to be measures which can increase the overall tax compliance and improve social norms. The first step is proposed to define the property rights that will separate business from the state. If some rights were appropriated unfairly the owners should pay out the residual price in form of taxes on the deferred basis. In this case the state won't be able to expropriate firms and the business won't need to secure its rights by the other means (bribery, political support).

Even if the society does not condone evasion anymore, it is business which pays taxes in Russia. Maybe in this respect the responsibility to pay taxes should also be on individual taxpayers since they play a crucial role in forming good social norms.

Bibliography

[1] Ahrend, R., Winograd, C. (2002) The Political Economy of Imperfect Taxation and Sustainable Privatization: When Do Countries Privatize and Who Gets the Spoils? Working Paper No. 2002-13, DELTA.

[2] Alexeev, M., Janeba, E., Osborne, S. (2004) Taxation and Evasion in the Presence of Extortion by Organized Crime, Journal of Comparative Economics 32, p.375-387.

[3] Allingham, M.G. and Sandmo, A. (1972) Income Tax Evasion: a Theoretical Analysis, Journal of Public Economics, 1, p. 323-338.

[4] Alm, J., Martinez-Vazquez, J., Torgler, B. (2005) Russian Attitudes Towards Paying Taxes - Before, During and After the Transition, Center for Research in Economics, Management and the Arts, Working Paper 27.

[5] Anderson, J.H., Gray, C.W. (2006) Anticorruption in Transition 3: Who is succeeding... and why? The World Bank.

[6] Andreoni, J., Erard, B., Feinstein, J. (1998) Tax Compliance, Journal of Economic Literature XXXVI, p. 818-860.

[7] Antel, S. (2003) Changes to the Tax System, International Tax Review, October.

[8] Bayer, R.-C., Cowell, F.A. (2006) Tax Compliance and Firms' Strategic Interdependence. DARP Working Paper, London School of Economics.

[9] Berkowitz, D., Li, W. (2000) Tax Rights in Transition Economies: a Tradegy of the Commons? Journal of Public Economics 76, p.369-397.

[10] Bird, R.M., Wallace, S. (2003) Is It Really so Hard to Tax the Hard-to-tax? The Content and Role of Presumptive Taxes, University of Toronto, Discussion Paper, December.

[11] Blackburn, K., Bose, N., Haque, M.E. (2005) The Incidence and Persistence of Corruption in Economic Development, forthcoming in Journal of Economic Dynamics and Control.

[12] Blood money: Corruption in Russia (2005), The Economist, 20 October 2005.

[13] Bond, S.R., Devereux, M.P. (1995) A Note on the Taxation of Capital Income and Economic Rents, Working Paper No. W95/18, The Institute for Fiscal Studies.

[14] Bond, S.R., Devereux, M.P. (1995) On the Design of a Neutral Business Tax under Uncertainty, Journal of Public Economics 58, p. 57-71.

[15] Bond, S.R., Devereux, M.P. (2003) Generalised R-based and S-based Taxes under Uncertainty, Journal of Public Economics 87, p. 1291-1311.

[16] Borck, R. (2004) Stricter Enforcement May Increase Tax Evasion, European Journal of Political Economy 20, p.725-737.

[17] Bordignon, M. (1993) A Fairness Approach to Income Tax Evasion, Journal of Public Economics 52, p.345-362.

[18] Bowles, R.A. (1999) Tax Policy, Tax Evasion and Corruption in Economies in Transition, in: Underground Economies in Transition (ed. Feige, E.L and Ott, K.), p. 67-100.

[19] Boycko, M., Shleifer, A., Vishny, R. (1996) A Theory of Privatization, The Economic Journal, 106 (March), p. 309-319.

[20] Boycko, M., Shleifer, A., Vishny, R. (1996) Second-best Economic Policy for a Divided Government, European Economic Review, 40, p. 767-774.

[21] Brealey, R., Myers, S. (2000) Principles of Corporate Finance, McGraw-Hill.

[22] Chen K.-P., Chu C.Y. (2005) Internal Control vs External Manipulation: a Model of Corporate Income Tax Evasion, Rand Journal of Economics, Spring, p.151-164.

[23] Chernyshov, S. (2005) Taxes - a Russian paradox, http://www.bdo.ru/eng/press/marketnews/?form=print??id=1903, last called on 24.03.2006.

[24] Coase, R.H. (1960) The Problem of Social Cost, Journal of Law and Economics, October.

[25] Concluding Statement of the IMF Mission to the Russian Federation (2004), Moscow, 24 June, 2004; http://www.imf.org/external/np/ms/2004/062404.htm, last called on 18.12.2005.

[26] Cowell, F.A. (1990) Cheating the Government: the Economics of Evasion, London: The MIT Press.

[27] Cowell, F.A. (2003) Sticks and Carrots, Discussion Paper prepared for the Conference on the Crisis in tax administration, The Brookings Institute, Washigton DC, Novermber 2002.

[28] Cremer, H. and Gahvari, F. (1993) Tax Evasion and Optimal Commodity Taxation, Journal of Public Economics, 50, p. 261-275.

[29] Cremer, H. and Gahvari, F. (1995) Tax Evasion and the Optimum General Income Tax, Journal of Public Economics 60, p. 235-249.

[30] Crocker, K.J., Slemrod, J.(2005) Corporate Tax Evasion with Agency Costs, Journal of Public Economics 89, Issue 9-10, p.1593-1610.

[31] Cule, M., Fulton, M. (2005) Some Implications of the Unofficial Economy - Bureaucratic Corruption Relationship in Transition Countries, Economics Letters 89, p.207-211.

[32] Cullis, J.G., Lewis, A. (1997) Why People Pay Taxes: from a Conventional Economic Model to a Model of Social Convention, Journal of Economic Psychology 18, p.305-321.

[33] Desai, M., Dyck, A., Zingales, L. (2004) Theft and Taxes, NBER Working Paper 10978, December.

[34] Douglas, R., Ellingsworth, P., McAndrews, J. (1996) What Management Expects: Evaluation of the Tax Department and its Executives, The Tax Executives, Jan.-Feb., p.29-32.

[35] Eilat, Y., Zinnes, C. (2000) The Shadow Economy in Tranition Countries: Consequences for Economic Growth and Donor Assistance, CAER II Discussion Paper No.83, September.

[36] Fedeli, S., Forte, F. (1999) Joint Income-Tax and VAT-Chain Evasion, European Journal of Political Economy 15, p. 391-415.

[37] Federal Budget Lost 2 bln.USD in Taxes from Oil Companies in 2004 (2005), News of Interfax, 30 November, 2005; http://www.interfax.ru/e/B/0/0.html?id issue=11428564, last called on 18.12 2005.

[38] Feige, E.L. (1999) Underground Economies in Transition: Noncompliance and Institutional Change, in: Underground Economies in Transition (ed. by Feige, E, and Ott, K.), Ashgate Publishing Ltd, p.11-27.

[39] Fjeldstad, O.-H., Tungodden, B. (2003) Fiscal Corruption: a Vice or a Virtue? World development 31, p.1459-1467.

[40] Fleischman, G., Herz, P. (2005) An Empirical Investigation of Trends in Barter Activity in the Russian Federation, The International Journal of Accounting 40, p.39-63.

[41] Franzoni, L.A. (1999) Tax Evasion and Tax Compliance, Working Paper, University of Bologna.

[42] Friedman, E., Johnson, S., Kaufmann, D., Zoido-Lobaton, P.(1999) Dodging the Grabing Hand: the Determinants of Unofficial Activity in 69 Countries, World Bank Discussion Paper.

[43] Gaddy, C., Ickes, B.W. (1998) A Simple Four Sector Model of Russia'a "Virtual" Economy, The Brookings Institution, Discussion Paper, October.

[44] Gerxhani, K. (2004) The Informal Sector in Developed and less Developed Countries: A Literature Survey, Public Choice, Vol 120, No. 3-4, p. 267-300.

[45] Gordon, J. (1989) Individual Morality and Reputation Costs as Deterrents to Tax Evasion, European Economic Review 33, p.797-805.

[46] Gordon, R. H., Bai, C., Li, D. (1999) Efficiency Losses from Tax Distortions vs. Government Control, European Economic Review, Vol. 43, p. 1095-1103.

[47] Gordon, R.H. and Nielsen, S.B. (1997) Tax Evasion in an Open Economy: Value-added vs. Income Taxation, Journal of Public Economics Vol. 66, p. 173-197.

[48] Grossman, G. (1982) The Second Economy of the USSR, in Tanzi, V. The Underground Economy in the United States and Abroad, Lexington DC.

[49] Gurvich, E. (2003) Optimal State: the Limit of Taxes' Reduction, Vedomosti, 16 June.

[50] Hainsworth, R., Tompson, W. (2002) Tax Policy and Tax Administration in Russia: the Case of the Banking Sector, Post-Communist Economies 14, p.277-300.

[51] Hare, P., Muravyev, A. (2002) Privatization in Russia, Reseach Paper, Russian-European Centre for Economic Policy, August.

[52] Hettich, W., Winer, S.L. (1988) Economic and Political Foundations of Tax Structure, American Economic Review 78, p.701-712.

[53] Hindriks, J., Keen, M., Muthoo, A. (1999) Corruption, Extortion, Evasion, Journal of Public Economics 74, p. 395-430.

[54] Hockley, G.C. (1992) Fiscal Policy: an Introduction. Routledge.

[55] Hoff, K., Stiglitz, J.E. (2002) After the Big Bang? Obstacles to the Emergence of the Rule of Law in Post-communist Societies, World Bank Policy Research Working Paper 2934, December.

[56] Ihrig, J., Moe, K.S. (2004) Lurking in the Shadows: the Informal Sector and Government Policy, Journal of Development Economics 73, p.541-557.

[57] Intergovernmental Fiscal Relations - International Experience and the Russian Reform, Fiscal Studies No.2, Deutsche Gesellschaft fuer Technische Zusammenarbeit, Eschborn.

[58] Ivanova, A., Keen, M. and Klemm, A. (2005) The Russian Flat Tax Reform, IMF Working Paper 05/16.

[59] Johnson, S., Kaufmann, D., Schleifer, A. (1997) The Unofficial Economy in Transition, Brookings Papers on Economic Activity 1997, p.159-221.

[60] Johnson, S., Kaufmann, D., Zoido-Lobaton, P. (1998) Regulatory Discretion and the Unofficial Economy, American Economic Review 88, Vol.2, May, p. 387-392.

[61] Kaufmann, D. (2001) Research on Corruption: Critical Empirical Issues, in: Jain A.K. (ed.) The Political Economy of Corruption, London, Routledge, p. 129-176.

[62] Kneen, P. (2000) Political Corruption in Russia and the Soviet Legacy, Crime, Law and Social Change 34, December, p.349-367.

[63] Kolm, S.-K. (1973) A Note on Optimum Tax Evasion, Journal of Public Economics 2, p.265-270.

[64] Krasilnikova, M. (2001) Introduction of a Flat Personal Income Tax and the Outlook for Legalization of Population Incomes, Research Paper, Russian-European Centre for Economic Policy, April.

[65] Laffont, J.-J., Martimort, D. (2002) The Theory of Incentives. The Principal-agent model. Princeton University Press.

[66] Lee, K. (1998) Tax Evasion, Monopoly, and Nonneutral Profit Taxes, National Tax Journal 51, p.333-338.

[67] Lieberman, I., Veimetra, R. (1996) The Rush for State Shares in the Klondyke of Wild East Capitalism: Loans-For-Shares Transactions in Russia, George Washington Journal of International Law and Economics, Vol. 29 No.3.

[68] Makedonskiy, S., (2005) Taxation Mechanisms Based on Simplified and Indirect Evaluation of Tax Liabilities, Russian-Euporean Center for Economic Policy, Moscow.

[69] Marrelli, M. (1984) On Indirect Tax Evasion, Journal of Public Economics, 25, p. 181-196.

[70] Marrelli, M and Martina, R. (1988) Tax Evasion and Strategic Behavior of the Firms, Journal of Public Economics, 37, p. 55-69.

[71] Martinez-Vazquez, J., McNab, R. (2000) The Tax Reform Experiment in Transitional Countries, Georgia State University, Working Paper, January.

[72] Mauro, P. (1998) Corruption and the Composition of Government Expenditure, Journal of Public Economics 69, p.263-279.

[73] Ministry of Taxation of the Russian Federation (2003) Overview: Progress of Tax Reform, International Tax Review, October 2003.

[74] Mitra, P., Stern, N. (2003) Tax Systems in Transition, Policy Research Working Paper 2947, World Bank, January.

[75] Mookherjee, D. and Png, I.P.L. (1995) Corruptible Law Enforcers: How Should They Be Compensated? The Economic Journal, Vol. 105, p. 145-159.

[76] Myles, G.D. (1995) Public Economics, Cambridge University Press.

[77] Myles, G.D. (2000) Wasteful Government, Tax Evasion, and the Provision of Public Goods, European Journal of Political Economy 16, p. 51-74.

[78] Myles, G.D., Naylor, R.A. (1996) A Model of Tax Evasion with Group Conformity and Social Customs, European Journal of Political Economy Vol. 12, p. 49-66.

[79] Newbery, D.M. (1997) Optimal Tax rates and Tax Design During Systemic Reform, Journal of Public Economics 63, p. 177-206.

[80] OECD Economic Surveys, Russian Federation (1997), Organisation for Economic Cooperation and Development, Paris.

[81] Panades, J. (2004) Tax Evasion and Relative Tax Contribution, Public Finance Review 32, No.2, March 2004.

[82] Panskov, V. (2003) Russian System of Taxation: the Problems of Development. Moscow, MZFER.

[83] Pirttilae, J. (1999) Tax Evasion and Economies in Transition: Lessons from Tax Theory, BOFIT Discussion Paper 2, Bank of Finland, Institute for economies in transition.

[84] Putin Keeps His Promise to Oligarchs, Initiates Tax Reforms (2005), MosNews, 28.03.2005; http://www.mosnews.com/news/2005/03/28/pubusiness.shtml, last called on 18.12.2005.

[85] Reinganum, J.F. and Wilde, L.L. (1985) Income Tax Compliance in a Principal-agent Framework, Journal of Public Economics 26, p.1-18.

[86] Reinganum, J.F. and Wilde, L.L. (1986) Equilibrium Verification and Reporting Policies in a Model of Tax Compliance, International Economic Review, Vol. 27, No. 3, p. 739-760.

[87] Rosefielde, S. (1998) Efficiency and Russia's Economic Recovery Potential to the Year 2000 and Beyond, Ashgate, Aldershot.

[88] Rosen, H. (2002) Public Finance, 6th ed., McGraw-Hill.

[89] Sachs, J., Zinnes, C., Eilat, Y. (2000) Patterns and Determinants of Economic Reform in Transition Countries, CAER II Discussion Paper No.61.

[90] Sandford, C. (2000) Why Tax Systems Differ: a Comparative Study of the Political Economy of Taxation, Fiscal Publications, Bath.

[91] Sandmo, A. (2004) The Theory of Tax Evasion: a Retrospective View, Norwegian School of Economics and Business Administation, November.

[92] Sappington, D. and Stiglitz, J. (1987) Privatization, Information and Incentives, NBER Working Paper 2196.

[93] Schmidt, K. (1990) The Costs and Benefits of Privatization, mimeo, MIT.

[94] Shapiro, C. and Willig, R. (1990) Economic Rationales for the Scope of Privatization, in: The Political Economy of Public Sector Reform and Privatization, London: Westview Press, p.55-87.

[95] Shleifer, A. and Vishny, R.W. (1993) Corruption, The Quarterly Journal of Economics, Vol. 108, p. 599-618.

[96] Schneider, F. and Enste, D. (2000) Shadow Economies: Size, Causes, and Consequences, Journal of Economic Literature Vol.XXXVIII, March, p. 77-114.

[97] Schneider, F., Enste, D. (2003) The Shadow Economy: An International Survey. Cambridge: Cambridge University Press.

[98] Slemrod, J., Yitzhaki, S. (2000) Tax Avoidance, Evasion, and Administration, NBER Working Paper 7473, January.

[99] States Within the State: Russia's Institutions Seem Designed to Ensure that Nothing Changes (2001), The Economist, 19 July 2001;

[100] Stiglitz, J. (2003) Globalization and Its Discontents, W.W.Norton and Company, New York.

[101] Tanzi, V. (2000) A Primer on Tax Evasion, in: Policies, Institutions and the Dark Side of Economics, Chentelham, Elgar, p. 171-185.

[102] Tanzi, V. (1998) Corruption Around the World: Causes, Consequences, Scope and Cures, IMF Staff Papers, Vol.45, No.4, December, p.559-594.

[103] Tanzi, V. (2000) Corruption Around the World, in: Policies, Institutions and the Dark Side of Economics, Chentelham, Elgar, p. 107-139.

[104] Tanzi, V. and Davoodi, H.R. (2000) Corruption, Growth, and Public Finances, IMF Working Paper 182.

[105] The Federal Bill "On the Federal Budget for 2005", 24 December 2004; http://www.budgetrf.ru/Publications/2005/Adoption/

Federal/ Npd/Budgetlaws/173fz231204/173fz231204 short.htm, last called on 18.12.2005.

[106] The Russian Tax Code, Part 2 (2000), Chapters 24-26; http://

mns.garant.ru/doc.jsp?urn=urn:garant:10800200, last called on 18.12.2005.

[107] Thiessen, U. (2003) The Impact of Fiscal Policy and Deregulation on Shadow Economies in Transition Countries: The Case of Ukraine, Public Choice 114, p. 295-318.

[108] Vasiljeva, A., Gurvich, E. (2004) The Structure of the Russian Tax System, Research Paper, Expert economic group.

[109] Vasiljeva, A., Gurvich, E., Subbotin, V. (2003) Analyzing the Tax Reform from an Economic Perspective, Voprosy Economiki 6.

[110] Vihanto, M. (2000) Tax Evasion in a Transition from Socialism to Capitalism: the Psychology of the Social Contract, BOFIT Discussion Papers 6.

[111] Virmani, A. (1989) Indirect Tax Evasion and Production Efficiency, Journal of Public Economics, 39, p. 223-237.

[112] Volvach, D., Shnurov, K. (2004) The Insurance Schemes of Tax Evasion: What the Experience Tells, The Russian Tax Courier 10.

[113] Wane, W. (2000) Tax Evasion, Corruption and the Renumeration of Heterogeneous Inspectors, Development Research Group, World Bank.

[114] Wang, L., Conant, L. (1988) Corporate Tax Evasion and Output Decisions of the Uncertain Monopolist, National Tax Journal, Vol. 41, No. 4, p.579-581.

[115] Wintrobe, R. (2001) Tax Evasion and Trust, University of Western Ontario, Discussion Paper, June.

[116] Yakovlev, A. (2001) Black Cash Tax Evasion in Russia: Its Forms, Incentives and Consequences at Firm Level, Europe-Asia Studies, Vol. 52, 2001, No.1, p. 1- 35.

[117] Yaniv, G. (1988) Withholding and Non-withheld Tax Evasion, Journal of Public Economics, 35, p. 183-204.

[118] Yeliseyeva, I. (2002) Measuring Shadow Economy at the Regional Level, Research Paper, Russian-European Centre for Economic Policy, May.

[119] Yoo, T., Hyun, J.K. (1998) International Comparison of the Black Economy: Empirical Evidence Using Micro-level Data, Unpublished Paper, presented at the 1998 Congress of the IIPF, Cordoba, Argentina.

[120] Zolotarevich, K., Pavlov, V. (2002) Rent For the State, Finansovij Kontrol 4, p. 68-73.

Jürgen G. Backhaus (ed.)

Essays on Fiscal Sociology

Frankfurt am Main, Berlin, Bern, Bruxelles, New York, Oxford, Wien, 2005.
VI, 277 pp., 4 fig., 6 tab.
Finanzsoziologie. Edited by Jürgen G. Backhaus. Vol. 1
ISBN 978-3-361-39967-9 · pb. € 39.80*

Due to the widespread dissatisfaction with the way fiscal sociology is being neglected while benefiting by its ever-growing importance, the volume *Essays on Fiscal Sociology* aims to provide a source, reference, and teaching supplement for the field of fiscal sociology. The essays comprised in this book were originally prepared for and read at the Erfurt Conferences on Fiscal Sociology. Please note that this conference is open to all researchers in this field internationally and it is taking place in the second week of October, before the semester starts.

Contents: Fiscal Sociology: What for? · States and the Crafting of Souls: Mind, Society, and Fiscal Sociology · Approaches to Fiscal Sociology · Public Finance and Welfare: From the Ignorance of the Veil to the Veil of Ignorance · Institutions, Entrepreneurship, and the Rationale of Government: An Outline of the Schumpeterian Theory of the State · Polycentric Public Finance and the Organization of Governance · Fiscal and Monetary Illusion and the Maastricht Rules · The Impact of Equity Driven Policy Measures on the Equity of the State · German Fiscal Sociology's Influence on Japan · Goldscheid's *Menschenökonomie* from a Modern Perspective · A Fiscal Sociological Theory of Tax Evasion on the Basis of Adam Smith and Otto Veit · Justi's Moral Economics and his System of Taxation (1766) · Fritz Karl Mann (1883–1979) · Critical Remarks on Joseph E. Stiglitz

Kolibri 360 GmbH
Ferdinand-Jühlke-Straße 7
99095 Erfurt, Deutschland
produktsicherheit@kolibri360.de

Druck:
CPI Druckdienstleistungen GmbH
im Auftrag der
Kolibri 360 GmbH
Ferdinand-Jühlke-Str. 7
99095 Erfurt